Vegan Instant Pot for Beginners

5-Ingredient Affordable, Quick and Healthy Plant-Based Recipes | Boost Your Energy, Heal Your Body and Live a Healthy lifestyle | 30-Day Meal Plan

Dr Robin Linus

© Copyright 2019 Dr Robin Linus - All Rights Reserved.

In no way is it legal to reproduce, duplicate, or transmit any part of this document by either electronic means or in printed format. Recording of this publication is strictly prohibited, and any storage of this material is not allowed unless with written permission from the publisher. All rights reserved.

The information provided herein is stated to be truthful and consistent, in that any liability, regarding inattention or otherwise, by any usage or abuse of any policies, processes, or directions contained within is the solitary and complete responsibility of the recipient reader. Under no circumstances will any legal liability or blame be held against the publisher for any reparation, damages, or monetary loss due to the information herein, either directly or indirectly.

Respective authors own all copyrights not held by the publisher.

Legal Notice:

This book is copyright protected. This is only for personal use. You cannot amend, distribute, sell, use, quote or paraphrase any part of the content within this book without the consent of the author or copyright owner. Legal action will be pursued if this is breached.

Disclaimer Notice:

Please note the information contained within this document is for educational and entertainment purposes only. Every attempt has been made to provide accurate, up-to-date and reliable, complete information. No warranties of any kind are expressed or implied. Readers acknowledge that the author is not engaging in the rendering of legal, financial, medical or professional advice.

By reading this document, the reader agrees that under no circumstances are we responsible for any losses, direct or indirect, which are incurred as a result of the use of information contained within this document, including, but not limited to, errors, omissions, or inaccuracies.

Table of Contents

Introduction 9

Chapter 1: Vegan Made Easy 10

    What is Veganism? 10

    Why Vegan? 11

    Benefits of a Vegan Diet 12

    Guidelines and Rules for Eating Vegan 13

    What to Eat 14

    What Not to Eat 15

    Tips for Success 16

Chapter 2: Instant Pot Basic 17

    What is the Instant Pot? 17

    Benefits of the Instant Pot 17

    How to use the Instant Pot 18

    Cleaning and Maintenance 19

    Useful Tips for Instant Pot 20

Chapter 3: 30-Day Meal Plan 21

Chapter 4: Breakfast and Brunch 28

    Oats 28

    Apple Spice Oats 29

Mushroom Risotto 30

Butternut Squash Risotto 31

Quinoa Burrito Bowls 32

Cilantro Lime Quinoa 33

Pumpkin Coffeecake Oatmeal 34

Breakfast Stuffed Sweet Potatoes 35

Breakfast Potatoes 36

Burritos 38

Chapter 5: Appetizers and Sides 39

Mashed Sweet Potatoes 39

Stuffed Acorn Squash 40

Cauliflower Tikka Masala 41

Mushroom Lettuce Wraps 42

Mac and Cheese 43

Brussels Sprouts 44

Artichokes 45

Green Beans 46

Asparagus with Garlic 47

Spicy Garlic Eggplant 48

Chapter 6: Soup, Stews and Chilies 49

Tomato Soup 49

Chili 50

Cream of Broccoli Soup 51

Spinach Soup 52

Black Bean Soup 53

Millet and Bean Chili 54

Vegetable Barley Soup 55

Potato Corn Chowder 56

Chickpea Potato Soup 57

Lentil Chili 58

Chapter 7: Beans and Grains 59

Millet Pilaf 59

Spiced Quinoa and Cauliflower Rice Bowls 60

Black Beans and Rice 62

Chickpea Curry 63

Split Pea Soup 64

Spanish Rice 65

Spiced Brown Rice 66

Salsa Brown Rice and Kidney Beans 67

Walnut Lentil Tacos 68

Citrusy Black Beans 69

Chapter 8: Vegetable Mains 70

Tofu Curry 70

Pumpkin Walnut Chili 71

Lentil Curry 72

Pasta Puttanesca 73

BBQ Meatballs 74

Lentil Sloppy Joes 75

Green Coconut Curry 76

Potato Carrot Medley 77

Jackfruit Curry 78

Potato Curry 79

Vegan Butter Chicken 80

Ratatouille 81

Chapter 9: Desserts and Beverages 82

Pear and Cranberry Cake 82

Peach Dump Cake 84

Apple Crisp 85

Carrot Cake 86

Double Chocolate Cake 88

  Pumpkin Spice Cake 90

  Brown Rice Pudding 91

  Baked Apples 92

Chapter 10: Sauces 93

  Jalapeno Hot Sauce 93

  Alfredo Sauce 94

  Buffalo Sauce 95

  Cheese Sauce 96

  Spaghetti Sauce 97

  Marinara Sauce 98

  Applesauce 99

  Hummus 100

Conclusion 101

Introduction

Veganism is becoming extremely popular. In recent years, many celebrities have adopted a vegan lifestyle, and grocery stores are now filled with vegan products. Veganism is a way of living having the goal of not to support animal exploitation, as much as possible, including all forms of exploitation, cruelty and unethical practices and treatment of animals for clothing, food, accessories, and any other purpose.

Anyone can follow a vegan lifestyle, be it kid, teens, or older adults. And, the best part, vegan is even healthy for nursing mother and pregnant women.

So, the first step is to learn the details of a vegan lifestyle and then to move on to its eating patterns, and what you can and can't eat on a vegan diet. And, this cookbook tells you everything you need to know about veganism.

Read on to know more.

Chapter 1: Vegan Made Easy

What is Veganism?

'Veganism' is a term coined in 1944 by a group of vegetarians who chose not to consume any dairy products like egg, milk, meat, and other animal product, as vegetarian do. Yes, so vegans share a lot of similarities with vegetarians, but vegan differs in one aspect which is completely excluding everything in the way of living which relates to animals. Hence, a vegan lifestyle excludes all form of animal product, be it food, clothing, or anything else as much as possible.

Vegan lifestyle includes:

- Dietary Vegans

Dietary vegans or plant-based eater don't consume the animal product in their food but continue using them in other lifestyle product like clothes and cosmetics.

- Whole food vegans

Just like the name suggests, the diet of these vegans is rich in whole foods such as veggies, fruits, nuts, seeds, legumes, and whole-grains.

- Raw food vegans

This group of vegans only eat foods that are raw or cooked below 118 degrees F of temperature.

- Low-fat vegans

These vegan limits high-fat foods in their diet such as coconut, avocado, and nuts. Instead, they rely on fruits and occasionally eat vegetables.

Why Vegan?

A vegan diet is not only about consuming plant-based products; it is so much more. There are many reasons why people go for a vegan lifestyle.

- Ethics

Vegans strongly believe that all living being has the right to free life. Therefore, vegans are conscious about ending a creature's life just for consuming their meat, drink its milk, or using their skin for clothes. Vegan strongly oppose the physical and psychological stress which animals have to endure for the sake of modern practices in farms like small cages and pens where livestock in farms. Due to this non-ethical behavior, vegan often speaks out against modern family methods such as force-feeding ducks, injecting livestock for more milk production, etc. Hence, ethical vegans show their opposition to ill-treatment for the animals by raising awareness about animal right and choosing products that don't use animals or their byproducts.

- Health

Many people turn to a vegan lifestyle for its positive impacts on health. For example, plant-based diets significantly reduce the risk of developing diabetes, cancer, and heart disease. Moreover, lowering the intake of animal product reduce chances of Alzheimer's diseases and death from heart disease or cancer. While some people choose veganism to avoid the side effect of hormones and antibiotics that are injected in animals due to modern animal agriculture. And, some people choose veganism to treat obesity, lower their body weight and body mass index.

- Environment

When people avoid animal products, this significantly impacts the environment culture of animal agriculture. It is found that animal product causes higher greenhouse gas emissions and require more resources than plant-based products. Animal agriculture is a water-intensive process and also leads to deforestation when forested areas are destroyed for the housing of livestock or pasture. The deforestation ultimately leads to habitat destruction and species and many species destruction. Moreover, chemicals and greenhouse emission contribute to climate change problems.

Benefits of a Vegan Diet

Nutritional benefits:

- Reduced saturated fats: Vegan diet has less saturated fats which improve health, especially when it comes to coronary diseases
- More energy: More carbs in a plant-based diet provide energy to the body
- Fiber: High fiber vegan diet leads to healthier bowel movement and help in fighting against colon cancer
- Anti-oxidants: Vegetables and fruits are rich in antioxidants that protect the body with some types of cancer
- Vitamins: Vitamins boost the immune system, heals wounds faster and benefit skin, eyes, brain, and heart.

Disease Prevention:

- Cardiovascular disease: Improve cardiovascular health and prevent heart attack and stroke
- Cholesterol: Eliminating animal foods means eliminating dietary cholesterol which improves heart health
- Blood pressure: Vegan diet is rich in whole foods which is beneficial in lowering

high blood pressure
- Cancer: Switching to a vegan diet reversed many illnesses like reducing chances of prostate cancer, colon cancer, and breast cancer
- Arthritis: Plant-based diet is very promising for improving health in individuals suffering from arthritis

Physical benefits

- Body mass index (BMI): Diet without meats lowers BMI which is an indicator of healthy weight loss
- Weight loss: Vegan diet eliminates unhealthy foods that tend to cause weight gain
- Healthy skin: Vitamins and other essential nutrients from vegetables makes skin healthy, so vegans have good healthy skin
- Longer life: Vegan lives three to six years longer than people who don't follow a vegan or vegetarian lifestyle
- Body odor: Eliminating meat and dairy product from diet reduce body odor, and body smells better
- Hairs and nails: Individuals who follow a vegan diet have strong hairs and healthier nails
- Migraines and allergies: Vegan diet is a relief from migraines and reduces allergy symptoms, runny nose, and congestion.

Guidelines and Rules for Eating Vegan

Rule # 1- Don't eat animal products

Vegan avoid all the animal products including meat, seafood, fish, poultry, dairy items, eggs, even gelatin, and honey. Bees produce honey and thus, it is an animal-based product. Instead of honey, use a natural sweetener like fruits, or those that are based on plants and trees such as maple syrup. Gelatin is made from the tendons and boiled bones of animals, and thus, vegan avoid gelatin. Gelatin is generally found in gummy candies, and Jell-o and its great alternate is agar-agar which is made from seaweed.

Rule #2 – Restaurant Guide

You will find the restaurant menu a bit tricky because it may be possible that even vegetarian food can be made with animal foods. For example, vegetable soup can be prepared with chicken broth, or pasta is made with eggs. Therefore, you may have to often ask about the ingredients before ordering your food. But, there are many vegan foods you can enjoy in a restaurant like stir-fries, chickpea curry, tofu fajitas.

What to Eat

Vegans can eat:

- All vegetables
- All fruits
- All herbs
- All beans
- All legumes
- All grains
- All seeds
- All nuts
- All spices
- Olive oil, coconut oil, avocado oil
- Soy-based products such as tofu and tempeh
- Whole-grain pasta
- Plant-based and nuts-based milk like coconut oil, almond milk, and rice milk

- Plant-based cheeses

What Not to Eat

Vegans cannot eat:

- Butter
- Cream
- Yogurt
- Cream cheese
- Ice cream
- Eggs from chicken, ostrich, quail
- Cheeses based on a cow or goat milk
- Milk from livestock
- Beef
- Poultry
- Wild meat
- Pork
- Veal
- Lamb
- Seafood
- Fish
- Honey and bees' products
- Gelatin
- Gelatin based beer and wine
- Caesar dressing made with anchovy paste
- Candies containing gelatin

- Deep-fried foods and French fries and fried in animal fat
- Pesto and sauce containing parmesan cheese
- Pasta containing eggs
- Dark chocolate containing milk fat and clarified butter

Tips for Success

- Fill your plate with a variety of foods such as soy foods, almond milk, greens, fruits, legumes, seeds, nuts, almond butter, orange juice, and sesame tahini
- Keep your vegan meal simple. Just find three to four whole food ingredients and make your food, this won't need more than basic cooking skills
- Replace an egg with half of mashed banana for bread, muffin, and pancakes
- Substitute cow's milk with rice milk, or soymilk in equal amounts for a smoothy, creamy soup, and pudding
- Use vegetable broth or stock instead of beef or chicken broth in pilaf, casserole, and soup
- Instead of ground beef for patties, burrito filling, taco meat, and spaghetti sauce, use soy crumbles
- Replace boiled eggs with firm tofu block for egg salads

Chapter2: Instant Pot Basic

What is the Instant Pot?

The instant pot is a small and versatile kitchen application featuring multi-purpose cooking methods. Yes, it can do the job of many cooking appliances such as pressure cooker, slow cooker, steamer, rice cooker, cake maker, yogurt maker, and more. Moreover, instant pot saves the counter space and money as it comes at a cheap price.

I am sure like anyone new to the instant pot; you must be skeptical that how one cooking appliance can be a steamer and yogurt maker. Well, the answer lies in the preset programs in the instant pot that are specifically designed to cook a variety of foods to perfections, whether it is rice, stew, cake, or yogurt. The basic programs in most of the models of instant pot are as followed:

- Slow cooker
- Steamer
- Pressure Cooker
- Rice Cooker
- Sauté/Browning/Simmering
- Warmer
- Yogurt Maker

Other models of instant pot also feature egg maker, sterilizer and cake maker.

Benefits of the Instant Pot

Take advantage of many benefits of instant pot

- Automatic cooking

Cooking in instant pot is fully automated. Instant pot switch to cooking cycle from preheating automatically and then in warming mood once cooking is done. And, since this whole process is automatic, this frees the cook from the hassle of monitoring cooking time and cooking temperature.

- Save timing and energy

Instant pot is an energy-efficient cooking appliance, second to microwave. The two major factors that contribute to this efficiency of the instant pot is its inner pot that is completely insulated and thus, doesn't need much energy to up. Secondly, instant pot requires less cooking liquid compare to traditional pressure-cooking methods, so it boils the food faster. The intelligent programming in the instant pot ensures that coking is consistent regardless of its volume.

- Retain nutrients and preserve taste

Boiling often tends to diminish the nutritional value of the food. With instant pot pressure cooking, the food is cooked quickly and evenly, and this allows the food to retain its nutrients up to 90 percent. Moreover, since food isn't exposed to air and cooked in steam, this allows food to retain its flavors and bright colors more profoundly.

How to use the Instant Pot

Here how you can use the instant pot in simple five steps
01 – Switch on the instant pot, insert inner pot, and set it to sauté/simmer mode. Add oil for greasing the inner pot, wait until it gets hot and then brown your vegetables or protein

like chicken or beef. You can also add herbs and spices to your food in instant pot in this step, too

02 – Press the cancel button, add remaining ingredients in the instant pot and set it to manual mode.

03 – Shut with its lid and make sure pressure valve is in sealing position. Tap the pressure button to set the instant pot at higher/low pressure and then hit + or – button to set the cooking time.

04 – Instant pot will take 10 minutes to build pressure, the red button will pop up indicating that pressure has built and then the countdown of cooking time will start

05 – The timer in the instant pot will beep when it is done will cooking and will switch to warm mode. Now, you can release pressure in two ways: manually or naturally. For natural pressure release, let lid stay in sealing position and wait for around 10 to 20 minutes or until the red button goes down which means the pressure is released. For quick pressure release, move the valve to venting position and let steam shoots out.

Cleaning and Maintenance

Step 1 – Take out the inner pot from the internal base, set it aside and now clean the base. Use a clean and damp kitchen towel, not wet, to wipe clean food debris in the inner base, its rim, and heating element

Step 2 – The real cooking is done in the inner pot, and that's why it is often charred, have stains, and hold the smell of food. You can simply soak the inner pot in a white vinegar solution for 5 minutes and then rinse it away. To get rid of stuck food in the inner pot, first, soak it in soapy warm water, then scrub it and rinse thoroughly.

Step 3 – Clear red floating and steam release value with any food debris or deposits.

Step 4 – Remove the silicone sealing ring from the lid and wash it in the dishwasher using a detergent at high-temperature cycle to completely remove odors in the ring.

Step 5 – Use a damp sponge to wipe the outside of the instant pot. You can also use a vinegar damp sponge to remove water stains or hard stains, followed by wiping with a damp paper towel.

Useful Tips for Instant Pot

Here are some tips that will help you with instant pot cooking:

- Always add at least half cup of liquid, broth or sauce, even if you want to keep pressure cooking simple. This will help in building pressure in the pot and quick food faster.
- Pressure will never build in the instant pot until the pressure valve is set to sealing position. Similarly, when you want to release pressure, move pressure valve to the venting position.
- Instant pot cooking doesn't require you soaking beans or legume or defrosting/thawing frozen ingredients. Just throw ingredients in any state and get started with the cooking.
- Know the instant pot cooking pot. If the recipe is indicating cooking time of 10 minutes, this time doesn't include pressure building time. Add 10 minutes of pressure building time to the cooking time and 10 to 15 minutes pressure releasing time if you have to release pressure naturally. In the end, the total instant pot cooking time gets to 30 minutes.

Chapter 3: 30-Day Meal Plan

Day 1

Breakfast: Oats

Lunch: Asparagus with Garlic

Dinner: Mushroom Lettuce Wraps

Dessert: Pear and Cranberry Cake

Day 2

Breakfast: Butternut Squash Risotto

Lunch: Chickpea Curry

Dinner: Tomato Soup

Dessert: Apple Crisp

Day 3

Breakfast: Quinoa Burrito Bowls

Lunch: Mashed Sweet Potatoes

Dinner: Millet Pilaf

Dessert: Double Chocolate Cake

Day 4

Breakfast: Breakfast Stuffed Sweet Potatoes

Lunch: Spicy Garlic Eggplant

Dinner: Chili

Dessert: Pumpkin Spice Cake

Day 5

Breakfast: Cilantro Lime Quinoa

Lunch: Split Pea Soup

Dinner: Spanish Rice

Dessert: Baked Apples

Day 6

Breakfast: Pumpkin Coffeecake Oatmeal

Lunch: Mac and Cheese

Dinner: Spiced Quinoa and Cauliflower Rice Bowls

Dessert: Carrot Cake

Day 7

Breakfast: Burritos

Lunch: Stuffed Acorn Squash

Dinner: Cream of Broccoli Soup

Dessert: Peach Dump Cake

Day 8

Breakfast: Apple Spice Oats

Lunch: Mashed Sweet Potatoes

Dinner: Walnut Lentil Tacos

Dessert: Double Chocolate Cake

Day 9

Breakfast: Mushroom Risotto

Lunch: Tofu Curry

Dinner: Spinach Soup

Dessert: Pear and Cranberry Cake

Day 10

Breakfast: Cilantro Lime Quinoa

Lunch: Pumpkin Walnut Chili

Dinner: Pasta Puttanesca

Dessert: Apple Crisp

Day 11

Breakfast: Breakfast Potatoes

Lunch: Brussels Sprouts

Dinner: Spiced Brown Rice

Dessert: Brown Rice Pudding

Day 12

Breakfast: Burritos

Lunch: BBQ Meatballs

Dinner: Black Bean Soup

Dessert: Baked Apples

Day 13

Breakfast: Breakfast Stuffed Sweet Potatoes

Lunch: Cauliflower Tikka Masala

Dinner: Black Beans and Rice

Dessert: Carrot Cake

Day 14

Breakfast: Pumpkin Coffeecake Oatmeal

Lunch: Chickpea Curry

Dinner: Tofu Curry

Dessert: Pumpkin Spice Cake

Day 15

Breakfast: Oats

Lunch: Split Pea Soup

Dinner: Millet and Bean Chili

Dessert: Peach Dump Cake

Day 16

Breakfast: Butternut Squash Risotto

Lunch: Brussels Sprouts

Dinner: Potato Carrot Medley

Dessert: Pear and Cranberry Cake

Day 17

Breakfast: Quinoa Burrito Bowls

Lunch: Pasta Puttanesca

Dinner: Salsa Brown Rice and Kidney Beans

Dessert: Apple Crisp

Day 18

Breakfast: Pumpkin Coffeecake Oatmeal

Lunch: Mashed Sweet Potatoes

Dinner: Vegetable Barley Soup

Dessert: Baked Apples

Day 19

Breakfast: Mushroom Risotto

Lunch: Lentil Curry

Dinner: Vegan Butter Chicken

Dessert: Double Chocolate Cake

Day 20

Breakfast: Cilantro Lime Quinoa

Lunch: Green Coconut Curry

Dinner: Pumpkin Walnut Chili

Dessert: Brown Rice Pudding

Day 21

Breakfast: Breakfast Stuffed Sweet Potatoes

Lunch: Lentil Sloppy Joes

Dinner: Potato Corn Chowder

Dessert: Pumpkin Spice Cake

Day 22

Breakfast: Apple Spice Oats

Lunch: Potato Curry

Dinner: Jackfruit Curry

Dessert: Peach Dump Cake

Day 23

Breakfast: Mushroom Risotto

Lunch: Mac and Cheese

Dinner: Chickpea Potato Soup

Dessert: Baked Apples

Day 24

Breakfast: Burritos

Lunch: BBQ Meatballs

Dinner: Mushroom Lettuce Wraps

Dessert: Apple Crisp

Day 25

Breakfast: Butternut Squash Risotto

Lunch: Spanish Rice

Dinner: Tofu Curry

Dessert: Pear and Cranberry Cake

Day 26

Breakfast: Cilantro Lime Quinoa

Lunch: Mashed Sweet Potatoes

Dinner: Lentil Curry

Dessert: Brown Rice Pudding

Day 27

Breakfast: Pumpkin Coffeecake Oatmeal

Lunch: Chickpea Curry

Dinner: Ratatouille

Dessert: Carrot Cake

Day 28

Breakfast: Breakfast Potatoes

Lunch: Cauliflower Tikka Masala

Dinner: Citrusy Black Beans

Dessert: Double Chocolate Cake

Day 29

Breakfast: Quinoa Burrito Bowls

Lunch: Green beans

Dinner: Green Coconut Curry

Dessert: Pumpkin Spice Cake

Day 30

Breakfast: Butternut Squash Risotto

Lunch: Lentil Sloppy Joes

Dinner: Lentil Chili

Dessert: Peach Dump Cake

Chapter 4: Breakfast and Brunch

Oats

Preparation time: 10 minutes
Cooking time: 4 minutes
Servings: 6

Ingredients:

- 2 cups oats, steel-cut
- 5 cups water

Method:

1. Switch on the instant pot, add oats and water in the inner pot and then secure instant pot with its lid in the sealed position.
2. Press the manual button, adjust cooking time to 4 minutes, select high-pressure cooking, and let cook until instant pot buzz.
3. Instant pot will take 10 minutes or more to build pressure, and when it buzzes, press the cancel button and do natural pressure release for 10 minutes or more until pressure knob drops down.
4. Then carefully open the instant pot, stir the oats and ladle into the bowls.
5. Serve oats with vegan milk and favorite topping.

Nutrition Value:

- Calories: 205 Cal
- Carbs: 35 g
- Fat: 3 g
- Protein: 8 g
- Fiber: 5 g

Apple Spice Oats

Preparation time: 10 minutes
Cooking time: 10 minutes
Servings: 4

Ingredients:

- 1 small apple, chopped
- 1 cup steel-cut oats
- 1/2 cup raisins
- 2 tablespoons maple syrup
- 1/2 cup applesauce, unsweetened

Method:

1. Switch on the instant pot, add oats in the inner pot, season with 1/4 teaspoon salt, 1 teaspoon cinnamon, and 1/2 teaspoon nutmeg and pour in applesauce and 3 cups water and stir until mixed.
2. Secure instant pot with its lid in the sealed position, then press the manual button, adjust cooking time to 10 minutes, select high-pressure cooking and let cook until instant pot buzz.
3. Instant pot will take 10 minutes or more to build pressure, and when it buzzes, press the cancel button and do natural pressure release for 10 minutes or more until pressure knob drops down.
4. Then carefully open the instant pot, stir the oats, add apples and raisins and stir until mixed.
5. Ladle oats into bowls, drizzle with maple syrup and serve.

Nutrition Value:

- Calories: 193 Cal
- Carbs: 40 g, Fat: 2 g
- Protein: 5 g
- Fiber: 6 g

Mushroom Risotto

Preparation time: 10 minutes
Cooking time: 25 minutes
Servings: 4

Ingredients:

- 1½ cups risotto rice
- 1 1/2-pound mixed mushrooms, stems discarded and chopped
- 1 tablespoon soy sauce
- ¼ cup cashew cream
- 4 cups vegetable broth

Method:

1. Switch on the instant pot, add 2 tablespoons oil in the inner pot, press the sauté/simmer button, then adjust cooking time to 5 minutes and let preheat.
2. Add mixed mushrooms, season with 1/8 teaspoon salt and 1/4 teaspoon black pepper and cook mushrooms for 10 minutes or until nicely golden brown.
3. Then add 1 teaspoon minced garlic, cook for 1 minute, add rice, stir well and cook for 3 minutes or until rice is slightly toasted.
4. Stir in soy sauce, cook for 2 minutes or until wine evaporates and then pour in reserved vegetable broth.
5. Press the cancel button, secure instant pot with its lid in the sealed position, then press the manual button, adjust cooking time to 5 minutes, select high-pressure cooking and let cook until instant pot buzz.
6. Instant pot will take 10 minutes or more to build pressure, and when it buzzes, press the cancel button and do quick pressure release until pressure knob drops down.
7. Then carefully open the instant pot, stir the risotto, add cashew cream, stir well and then garnish with parsley.
8. Serve straight away.

Nutrition Value:

- Calories: 243 Cal
- Carbs: 30 g, Fat: 9.8 g
- Protein: 7.6 g
- Fiber: 0.9 g

Butternut Squash Risotto

Preparation time: 5 minutes
Cooking time: 16 minutes
Servings: 8

Ingredients:

- 2 cups Arborio rice
- 4 cups butternut squash, peeled, seeded and diced
- 5-ounces baby spinach
- 8-ounce Baby Bella mushrooms, sliced
- 4 cups vegetable broth

Method:

1. Switch on the instant pot, pour water in the inner pot, press the sauté/simmer button, then adjust cooking time to 5 minutes and let preheat.
2. Add squash, stir well and continue cook for 2 minutes.
3. Then add mushrooms, cook for another minute, add 1 tablespoon minced garlic, stir well and cook for 3 minutes.
4. Then add rice, stir until combined, season rice with 1 teaspoon salt, 1/3 teaspoon black pepper and 1/4 teaspoon Italian seasoning.
5. Pour in the broth, stir well to remove browned bits from the bottom of the pot and press the cancel button.
6. Top rice mixture with spinach, then secure instant pot with its lid in the sealed position, press the manual button, adjust cooking time to 6 minutes, select high-pressure cooking and let cook until instant pot buzz.
7. Then slowly blend in water until pesto is blended to desired consistency.
8. When instant pot buzzes, press the cancel button and do quick pressure release until pressure knob drops down.
9. Then carefully open the instant pot, stir risotto, transfer into bowls and serve.
10. Serve the risotto with pesto.

Nutrition Value:

- Calories: 342.810 Cal
- Carbs: 58 g
- Fat: 9.1 g
- Protein: 9 g
- Fiber: 3.7 g

Quinoa Burrito Bowls

Preparation time: 10 minutes
Cooking time: 26 minutes
Servings: 4

Ingredients:

- 1 cup quinoa, rinsed
- 1 1/2 cups cooked black beans
- 1/2 of medium red onion, peeled and diced
- 1 medium bell pepper, cored and diced
- 1 cup tomato salsa, and more for serving

Method:

1. Switch on the instant pot, grease the inner pot with 1 teaspoon olive oil, press the sauté/simmer button, then adjust cooking time to 5 minutes and let preheat.
2. Add onion and pepper and cook for 8 minutes or until softened, then season with 1/2 teaspoon salt and 1 teaspoon ground cumin and cook for 1 minute or until fragrant.
3. Add quinoa and beans, then pour in salsa and 1 cup water, stir until mixed and press the cancel button.
4. Secure instant pot with its lid in the sealed position, then press the rice button, adjust cooking time to 12 minutes, select low-pressure cooking and let cook until instant pot buzz.
5. Instant pot will take 10 minutes or more to build pressure, and when it buzzes, press the cancel button and do natural pressure release for 10 minutes or more until pressure knob drops down.
6. Then carefully open the instant pot, fluff quinoa with a fork and ladle into bowls.
7. Serve with guacamole, salsa, and lemon wedges.

Nutrition Value:

- Calories: 657.7 Cal
- Carbs: 95 g
- Fat: 17.4 g
- Protein: 34.1 g
- Fiber: 25.8 g

Cilantro Lime Quinoa

Preparation time: 10 minutes
Cooking time: 5 minutes
Servings: 4

Ingredients:

- 1 1/2 cups quinoa
- 4-ounce green chilies
- 1/2 of white onion, peeled and chopped
- 1/2 bunch of cilantro
- 1 1/2 cups vegetable broth

Method:

1. Place onions in a food processor, add chilies and cilantro and pulse for 1 minute or until smooth.
2. Switch on the instant pot, tip the onion mixture into the inner pot, season with 1 teaspoon salt and ½ teaspoon black pepper and stir until mixed.
3. Secure instant pot with its lid in the sealed position, then press the manual button, adjust cooking time to 5 minutes, select high-pressure cooking and let cook until instant pot buzz.
4. Instant pot will take 10 minutes or more to build pressure, and when it buzzes, press the cancel button and do natural pressure release for 10 minutes or more until pressure knob drops down.
5. Then carefully open the instant pot, fluff the quinoa and ladle into bowls.
6. Drizzle with lime juice and serve.

Nutrition Value:

- Calories: 550 Cal
- Carbs: 66 g
- Fat: 25 g
- Protein: 17 g
- Fiber: 3 g

Pumpkin Coffeecake Oatmeal

Preparation time: 10 minutes
Cooking time: 3 minutes
Servings: 6

Ingredients:

- 1 1/2 cups oats, steel-cut
- 2 teaspoons cinnamon
- 1 teaspoon allspice
- 1 teaspoon vanilla extract, unsweetened
- 1 1/2 cups pumpkin puree

Method:

1. Switch on the instant pot, place all the ingredients in the inner pot, pour in 4 1/2 cups water and stir until mixed.
2. Secure instant pot with its lid in the sealed position, then press the manual button, adjust cooking time to 3 minutes, select high-pressure cooking and let cook until instant pot buzz.
3. When instant pot buzzes, press the cancel button and do natural pressure release for 10 minutes or more until pressure knob drops down.
4. Then carefully open the instant pot, stir the oats and serve straight away.

Nutrition Value:

- Calories: 254 Cal
- Carbs: 45 g
- Fat: 5 g
- Protein: 7 g
- Fiber: 7 g

Breakfast Stuffed Sweet Potatoes

Preparation time: 10 minutes
Cooking time: 15 minutes
Servings: 4

Ingredients:

- 2 tablespoons blueberries, fresh
- 1 medium sweet potato
- 1 tablespoon chopped pecans
- 1 tablespoon maple syrup
- 1 tablespoon almond butter

Method:

1. Switch on the instant pot, pour in 1 cup water, insert steamer basket and place sweet potatoes on it.
2. Secure instant pot with its lid in the sealed position, then press the manual button, adjust cooking time to 15 minutes, select high-pressure cooking and let cook until instant pot buzz.
3. Instant pot will take 10 minutes or more to build pressure, and when it buzzes, press the cancel button and do natural pressure release for 10 minutes or more until pressure knob drops down.
4. Carefully open the instant pot, take out the sweet potatoes, and let rest until cool enough to handle.
5. Then cut the sweet potato, use a fork to mash its flesh and then drizzle with butter and maple syrup.
6. Sprinkle potatoes with berries and pecans and serve.

Nutrition Value:

- Calories: 369 Cal
- Carbs: 50 g
- Fat: 17 g
- Protein: 7 g
- Fiber: 8 g

Breakfast Potatoes

Preparation time: 10 minutes
Cooking time: 35 minutes
Servings: 5

Ingredients:

- 6 medium potatoes, peeled and ½-inch cubed
- 1 medium white onion, peeled and ½-inch cubed
- 1 medium green bell pepper, ½-inch cubed
- 3/4 cup vegetable broth

Method:

1. Switch on the instant pot, add 3 tablespoons coconut oil in the inner pot, press the sauté/simmer button, then adjust cooking time to 5 minutes and let preheat.
2. Then add potatoes and cook for 3 minutes or until sauté.
3. Sprinkle potatoes with ¾ teaspoon salt, 1/3 teaspoon black pepper, ¼ teaspoon paprika and 1 tablespoon nutritional yeast, cook for 4 minutes and then press the cancel button.
4. Secure instant pot with its lid in the sealed position, then press the manual button, adjust cooking time to 1 minute, select high-pressure cooking and let cook until instant pot buzz.
5. Instant pot will take 10 minutes or more to build pressure, and when it buzzes, press the cancel button and do quick pressure release until pressure knob drops down.
6. Carefully open the instant pot, gently stir the potatoes, then transfer into a bowl and let refrigerate until cooked.
7. Then place a skillet pan over medium heat, grease with oil and when hot, add onion and pepper and cook for 10 minutes or until softened.
8. Transfer vegetables to a plate, add potatoes into the pan and cook for 10 to 15 minutes or until potatoes are crispy and nicely browned.
9. Return vegetables into the pan, stir well and cook for 1 minute or until thoroughly heated.
10. Serve immediately.

Nutrition Value:

- Calories: 157 Cal
- Carbs: 30 g
- Fat: 2.5 g

- Protein: 4.6 g
- Fiber: 9 g

Burritos

Preparation time: 10 minutes
Cooking time: 32 minutes
Servings: 6

Ingredients:

- 15-ounces cooked black beans
- 1 1/2 cups brown rice, uncooked
- 1 cup chopped kale
- 1 medium red bell pepper, diced
- 12-ounce tomato salsa

Method:

1. Switch on the instant pot, grease the inner pot with 3 tablespoons oil, press the sauté/simmer button, then adjust cooking time to 5 minutes and let preheat.
2. Add bell pepper and 1 ½ teaspoon garlic, cook for 3 minutes, then add remaining ingredients for the burrito filling, season with 1 teaspoon salt, 2 teaspoon red chili powder, 1 teaspoon paprika, 1 teaspoon cumin and stir until mixed.
3. Pour in 2 cups water, then press the cancel button, secure instant pot with its lid in the sealed position, press the manual button, adjust cooking time to 24 minutes, select high-pressure cooking and let cook until instant pot buzz.
4. Instant pot will take 10 minutes or more to build pressure, and when it buzzes, press the cancel button and do natural pressure release for 10 minutes or more until pressure knob drops down.
5. Then carefully open the instant pot, stir the mixture and taste to adjust seasoning.
6. Spoon the mixture evenly on tortillas, top with lettuce, avocado, and cheese and serve with salsa.

Nutrition Value:

- Calories: 491 Cal
- Carbs: 70 g
- Fat: 16 g
- Protein: 21 g
- Fiber: 10 g

Chapter 5: Appetizers and Sides

Mashed Sweet Potatoes

Preparation time: 10 minutes
Cooking time: 15 minutes
Servings: 8

Ingredients:

- 3 pounds sweet potatoes, peeled and 2-inch cubed
- 6 cloves of garlic, peeled
- 1 teaspoon ground black pepper
- 1/2 teaspoon chopped rosemary
- 1/4 cup coconut milk

Method:

1. Switch on the instant pot, pour 1 cup water in the inner pot, insert steamer rack and place sweet potatoes and season with 1/8 teaspoon salt and garlic.
2. Secure instant pot with its lid in the sealed position, then press the manual button, adjust cooking time to 15 minutes, select high-pressure cooking and let cook until instant pot buzz.
3. Instant pot will take 10 minutes or more to build pressure, and when it buzzes, press the cancel button and do quick pressure release until pressure knob drops down.
4. Then carefully open the instant pot, take out the sweet potatoes, place them in a large bowl, and mash with a fork.
5. Add remaining ingredients, mash well until creamy and serve.

Nutrition Value:

- Calories: 204 Cal
- Carbs: 36 g
- Fat: 5 g
- Protein: 3 g
- Fiber: 5 g

Stuffed Acorn Squash

Preparation time: 10 minutes
Cooking time: 5
Servings: 3

Ingredients:

- 15-ounce cooked chickpeas
- 1/3 cup dried cranberries
- 3 small acorn squashes, each about 1 pound, destemmed and deseeded
- 8 ounces cremini mushrooms, chopped
- 1 medium shallot, peeled and chopped

Method:

1. Switch on the instant pot, pour the ½ cup water in the inner pot, insert a trivet stand and place squash on it, cut side up.
2. Secure instant pot with its lid in the sealed position, then press the manual button, adjust cooking time to 4 minutes, select high-pressure cooking and let cook until instant pot buzz.
3. Instant pot will take 10 minutes or more to build pressure, and when it buzzes, press the cancel button, do natural pressure release for 5 minutes and then do quick pressure release until pressure knob drops down.
4. Meanwhile, place a skillet over medium heat, add 1 tablespoon oil and when hot, add shallots and cook for 4 minutes, then add 1 tablespoon minced garlic, cook for 30 seconds until fragrant.
5. Then season with 1 teaspoon salt, add 1/2 teaspoon black pepper, add mushrooms and cook for 5 minutes or more until mushrooms are nicely brown.
6. Add remaining ingredients, stir well and cook for 2 minutes.
7. When squash is cooked, open the instant pot and transfer squash on a baking sheet.
8. Stuff squash with hot rice mixture and serve immediately.

Nutrition Value:

- Calories: 256 Cal
- Carbs: 47 g
- Fat: 4 g
- Protein: 7 g
- Fiber: 7 g

Cauliflower Tikka Masala

Preparation time: 10 minutes
Cooking time: 15 minutes
Servings: 4

Ingredients:

- 4 cups cauliflower florets
- 3 cups diced tomatoes
- 1 tablespoon maple syrup
- ½ cup tomato juice
- 1/2 cup cashew cream

Method:

1. Switch on the instant pot, grease the inner pot with 1 tablespoon olive oil, press the sauté/simmer button, then adjust cooking time to 5 minutes and let preheat.
2. Add ½ cup diced onion, 1 ½ teaspoon minced ginger, and 1 tablespoon grated garlic, cook for 5 minutes or until onions are caramelized, then season with 1/2 teaspoon salt, 1/2 teaspoon red chili powder, 1 teaspoon turmeric, and 2 teaspoons dried fenugreek leaves, stir well and cook for 2 minutes.
3. Stir in water to remove browned bits from the bottom of pots, then add remaining ingredients except for cream and stir until mixed.
4. Press the cancel button, secure instant pot with its lid in the sealed position, then press the manual button, adjust cooking time to 2 minutes, select high-pressure cooking and let cook until instant pot buzz.
5. Instant pot will take 10 minutes or more to build pressure, and when it buzzes, press the cancel button, do natural pressure release for 2 minutes and then do quick pressure release until pressure knob drops down.
6. Then carefully open the instant pot, stir in cashew cream until mixed and serve.

Nutrition Value:

- Calories: 196 Cal
- Carbs: 35.1 g
- Fat: 3.8 g
- Protein: 9.6 g
- Fiber: 12.5 g

Mushroom Lettuce Wraps

Preparation time: 25 minutes
Cooking time: 25 minutes
Servings: 6

Ingredients:

- 1-pound Portobello mushrooms, halved and sliced
- 2 tablespoons chili sauce
- ¼ cup maple syrup
- ¼ cup soy sauce
- 2 tablespoons apple cider vinegar

Method:

1. Switch on the instant pot, grease the inner pot with 2 tablespoons sesame oil, pour in ¼ cup water, then place all the ingredients, stir all the ingredients until just mixed and let sit for 15 minutes.
2. Secure instant pot with its lid in the sealed position, then press the manual button, adjust cooking time to 20 minutes, select high-pressure cooking and let cook until instant pot buzz.
3. Instant pot will take 10 minutes or more to build pressure, and when it buzzes, press the cancel button and do natural pressure release for 10 minutes or more until pressure knob drops down.
4. Then carefully open the instant pot, stir the mixture and press the sauté/simmer button.
5. Stir together 1 tablespoon cornstarch and 2 tablespoons water until smooth, add into the instant pot, stir well and cook for 5 minutes or until sauce reach to desired consistency.
6. Garnish with green onions and sesame seeds, then place in lettuce leaves and serve.

Nutrition Value:

- Calories: 161 Cal
- Carbs: 33 g
- Fat: 3 g
- Protein: 6 g
- Fiber: 6 g

Mac and Cheese

Preparation time: 10 minutes
Cooking time: 15 minutes
Servings: 4

Ingredients:

- 16-ounce whole-grain macaroni, uncooked
- 2 tablespoons vegan butter
- 2 cups grated vegan parmesan cheese
- 1/2 cup cashew cream

Method:

1. Switch on the instant pot, add pasta into the inner pot, season with 1 teaspoon salt and pour in 4 cups vegetable stock.
2. Secure instant pot with its lid in the sealed position, then press the manual button, adjust cooking time to 4 minutes, select high-pressure cooking and let cook until instant pot buzz.
3. Instant pot will take 10 minutes or more to build pressure, and when it buzzes, press the cancel button and do natural pressure release for 10 minutes or more until pressure knob drops down.
4. Then carefully open the instant pot, stir the pasta, add remaining ingredients, season with 1/8 teaspoon paprika and 2 tablespoons nutritional yeast and stir well until incorporated and cheese melts.
5. Serve immediately.

Nutrition Value:

- Calories: 270.8 Cal
- Carbs: 50 g
- Fat: 3.3 g
- Protein: 14.4 g
- Fiber: 8.8 g

Brussels Sprouts

Preparation time: 5 minutes
Cooking time: 12 minutes
Servings: 5

Ingredients:

- 3 tablespoons chopped tomatoes, sun-dried
- 1-pound Brussels sprouts, trimmed and halved
- 1 teaspoon olive oil
- 3 tablespoons soy sauce
- 3 tablespoons apple cider vinegar

Method:

1. Switch on the instant pot, grease the inner pot, press the sauté/simmer button, then adjust cooking time to 5 minutes and let preheat.
2. Add sprouts, cook for 3 minutes or until heated, then drizzle with soy sauce and vinegar and toss until coated.
3. Press the cancel button, secure instant pot with its lid in the sealed position, then press the manual button, adjust cooking time to 4 minutes, select high-pressure cooking and let cook until instant pot buzz.
4. Instant pot will take 10 minutes or more to build pressure, and when it buzzes, press the cancel button and do quick pressure release until pressure knob drops down.
5. Then carefully open the instant pot, stir in tomatoes until mixed and serve.

Nutrition Value:

- Calories: 62 Cal
- Carbs: 10 g
- Fat: 1 g
- Protein: 4 g
- Fiber: 3 g

Artichokes

Preparation time: 5 minutes
Cooking time: 8 minutes
Servings: 2

Ingredients:

- 2 artichokes, about ½ pound
- 2 tablespoons minced garlic
- 2 tablespoons vegan butter
- ¼ teaspoon salt
- 1 lemon, juiced

Method:

1. Cut the stem from each artichoke and trim the tip about 1-inch.
2. Switch on the instant pot, pour 1 cup cold water in the inner pot, insert steamer basket, then place artichokes on it and drizzle with lemon juice.
3. Secure instant pot with its lid in the sealed position, then press the manual button, adjust cooking time to 8 minutes, select high-pressure cooking and let cook until instant pot buzz.
4. Instant pot will take 10 minutes or more to build pressure, and when it buzzes, press the cancel button and do quick pressure release until pressure knob drops down.
5. Meanwhile, prepare garlic dip and for this, place a saucepan over medium-low heat, add butter and when it melts, add garlic and cook for 1 minute or until brown and fragrant.
6. Remove saucepan from the heat, season the mixture with salt and set aside until required.
7. Then carefully open the instant pot, take out artichoke hearts and serve with garlic dip.

Nutrition Value:

- Calories: 270 Cal
- Carbs: 34.5 g
- Fat: 12.1 g
- Protein: 11 g
- Fiber: 17.6 g

Green Beans

Preparation time: 5 minutes
Cooking time: 2 minutes
Servings: 4

Ingredients:

- 1-pound green beans, fresh
- ½ teaspoon minced garlic
- 2 tablespoons vegan butter
- 1 cup water

Method:

1. Switch on the instant pot, pour water in the inner pot and insert steamer basket.
2. Place beans in the heatproof bowl that fits into instant pot, season beans with ¾ teaspoon salt and ½ teaspoon black pepper, add garlic and butter and then place bowl on the trivet stand.
3. Secure instant pot with its lid in the sealed position, then press the manual button, adjust cooking time to 2 minutes, select low-pressure cooking and let cook until instant pot buzz.
4. Instant pot will take 10 minutes or more to build pressure, and when it buzzes, press the cancel button and do natural pressure release for 10 minutes or more until pressure knob drops down.
5. Then carefully open the instant pot, take out the bowl and serve.

Nutrition Value:

- Calories: 2.2 Cal
- Carbs: 0.5 g
- Fat: 0 g
- Protein: 0.1 g
- Fiber: 0.2 g

Asparagus with Garlic

Preparation time: 10 minutes
Cooking time: 6 minutes
Servings: 4

Ingredients:

- 2 bunches of asparagus, hard ends trimmed off
- ½ teaspoon minced garlic
- 1 teaspoon lemon zest
- 3 tablespoons olive oil
- ½ lemon, juiced

Method:

1. Switch on the instant pot, pour 1 cup water in the inner pot, insert a trivet stand and place asparagus on it.
2. Secure instant pot with its lid in the sealed position, then press the steam button, adjust cooking time to 0 minutes, select low-pressure cooking and let cook until instant pot buzz.
3. Instant pot will take 10 minutes or more to build pressure, and when it buzzes, press the cancel button and do quick pressure release until pressure knob drops down.
4. Then carefully open the instant pot, transfer asparagus to a serving platter, and set aside.
5. Drain the instant pot, press the sauté/simmer button, adjust cooking time to 5 minutes and when hot, add oil along with garlic and lemon zest and cook for 1 minute or until fragrant.
6. Then add asparagus, season with ½ teaspoon salt and ½ teaspoon black pepper, drizzle with lemon juice and stir until mixed.
7. Serve straight away.

Nutrition Value:

- Calories: 94 Cal
- Carbs: 4.7 g
- Fat: 8.6 g
- Protein: 2 g
- Fiber: 2 g

Spicy Garlic Eggplant

Preparation time: 5 minutes
Cooking time: 10 minutes
Servings: 4

Ingredients:

- 1 medium eggplant, destemmed and 1-inch cubed
- 1 teaspoon garlic powder
- ½ teaspoon red pepper
- 2 tablespoons olive oil
- ¼ cup tomato sauce

Method:

1. Switch on the instant pot, pour ½ cup water in the inner pot, and add eggplant pieces.
2. Secure instant pot with its lid in the sealed position, then press the manual button, adjust cooking time to 5 minutes, select high-pressure cooking and let cook until instant pot buzz.
3. Instant pot will take 10 minutes or more to build pressure, and when it buzzes, press the cancel button and do quick pressure release until pressure knob drops down.
4. Then carefully open the instant pot, drain the eggplant, and set aside.
5. Drain the inner pot, press the sauté/simmer button, adjust cooking time to 5 minutes and when hot, add oil and eggplant pieces.
6. Season with red pepper, ½ teaspoon Italian seasoning, 1 teaspoon salt, and 1 teaspoon sweet paprika, stir until combined and cook for 5 minutes.
7. Serve straight away.

Nutrition Value:

- Calories: 520 Cal
- Carbs: 68.8 g
- Fat: 16.6 g
- Protein: 15.4 g
- Fiber: 10 g

Chapter 6: Soup, Stews and Chilies

Tomato Soup

Preparation time: 10 minutes
Cooking time: 15 minutes
Servings: 5

Ingredients:

- 2-pounds tomatoes, quartered
- 1 cup chopped carrots
- 2 tablespoons nutritional yeast
- 2 tablespoons tomato paste
- 1 tablespoon apple cider vinegar

Method:

1. Switch on the instant pot, grease the inner pot with 1 tablespoon olive oil, press the sauté/simmer button, then adjust cooking time to 5 minutes and let preheat.
2. Add tomato, carrot and 3 tablespoons minced garlic, cook for 3 minutes or until vegetables begin to soften, then add remaining ingredients, pout in 1 cup vegetable stock and stir until mixed.
3. Press the cancel button, secure instant pot with its lid in the sealed position, then press the manual button, adjust cooking time to 10 minutes, select high-pressure cooking and let cook until instant pot buzz.
4. Instant pot will take 10 minutes or more to build pressure, and when it buzzes, press the cancel button and do natural pressure release for 10 minutes or more until pressure knob drops down.
5. Then carefully open the instant pot, stir the mixture and puree using an immersion blender until smooth.
6. Ladle soup into bowls and serve.

Nutrition Value:

- Calories: 102 Cal
- Carbs: 14 g
- Fat: 2 g
- Protein: 4 g
- Fiber: 4 g

Chili

Preparation time: 10 minutes
Cooking time: 25 minutes
Servings: 4

Ingredients:

- 30-ounce red kidney beans, cooked
- 15-ounce diced tomatoes
- 1 small white onion, peeled and sliced
- 4 cups sweet potatoes, peeled and ½-inch cubed
- 2 tablespoons maple syrup

Method:

1. Switch on the instant pot, grease the inner pot with 1 tablespoon olive oil, press the sauté/simmer button, then adjust cooking time to 5 minutes and let preheat.
2. Add onion, cook for 5 minutes or until sauté, then add 1 teaspoon minced garlic and cook for 1 minute or until fragrant.
3. Add remaining ingredients, season with 1 ½ teaspoon salt, ¾ teaspoon ground black pepper, 1 ½ tablespoons red chili powder, ¼ teaspoon cayenne pepper, pour in 2 cups vegetables broth and stir until mixed.
4. Press the cancel button, secure instant pot with its lid in the sealed position, then press the soup button, adjust cooking time to 15 minutes, select high-pressure cooking and let cook until instant pot buzz.
5. Instant pot will take 10 minutes or more to build pressure, and when it buzzes, press the cancel button and do natural pressure release for 10 minutes or more until pressure knob drops down.
6. Then carefully open the instant pot, stir the chili and garnish with green onions.
7. Serve straight away.

Nutrition Value:

- Calories: 239 Cal
- Carbs: 40 g
- Fat: 4 g
- Protein: 3 g
- Fiber: 5 g

Cream of Broccoli Soup

Preparation time: 10 minutes
Cooking time: 15 minutes
Servings: 4

Ingredients:

- 5 cups broccoli florets
- 1 cup carrots, diced
- 1/3 cup cashews
- 1 cup diced white onion
- 3/4 cup coconut milk

Method:

1. Switch on the instant pot, grease the inner pot with 1 tablespoon olive oil, press the sauté/simmer button, then adjust cooking time to 5 minutes and let preheat.
2. Add onion and 1 ½ teaspoon minced garlic, cook for 3 minutes, then add remaining ingredients except for coconut milk, season with 1 ½ teaspoon salt and ¾ teaspoon black pepper and stir until just mixed.
3. Pour in 2 cups vegetable stock, press the cancel button, secure instant pot with its lid in the sealed position, then press the manual button, adjust cooking time to 3 minutes, select high-pressure cooking and let cook until instant pot buzz.
4. Instant pot will take 10 minutes or more to build pressure, and when it buzzes, press the cancel button and do natural pressure release for 10 minutes or more until pressure knob drops down.
5. Then carefully open the instant pot, pour in coconut milk, then puree the soup until smooth and creamy.
6. Drizzle with lemon juice and serve.

Nutrition Value:

- Calories: 265 Cal
- Carbs: 21 g
- Fat: 18 g
- Protein: 9 g
- Fiber: 4 g

Spinach Soup

Preparation time: 10 minutes
Cooking time: 15 minutes
Servings: 8

Ingredients:

- 5-ounce baby spinach
- 3 cups broccoli florets
- 1 small bunch of kale, destemmed and chopped
- 1 medium white onion, peeled and diced
- 2 cups coconut milk

Method:

1. Switch on the instant pot, grease the inner pot with 1 tablespoon coconut oil, press the sauté/simmer button, then adjust cooking time to 5 minutes and let preheat.
2. Add onion and 1 ½ tablespoon minced garlic, season with 1 teaspoon salt, ½ teaspoon ground black pepper, 1/2 teaspoon paprika and 1/2 teaspoon cumin and cook for 5 minutes or until onions caramelize.
3. Add broccoli and kale, pour in 6 cups vegetable stock and press the cancel button.
4. Secure instant pot with its lid in the sealed position, then press the manual button, adjust cooking time to 5 minutes, select high-pressure cooking and let cook until instant pot buzz.
5. Instant pot will take 10 minutes or more to build pressure, and when it buzzes, press the cancel button and do quick pressure release until pressure knob drops down.
6. Then carefully open the instant pot, add spinach, stir well and then puree the soup until smooth.
7. Press the sauté/simmer button, then adjust cooking time to 5 minutes, stir in coconut milk and let cool.
8. Ladle soup into bowls and serve.

Nutrition Value:

- Calories: 321.5 Cal
- Carbs: 18 g
- Fat: 26 g
- Protein: 6.8 g
- Fiber: 2.5 g

Black Bean Soup

Preparation time: 10 minutes
Cooking time: 40 minutes
Servings: 6

Ingredients:

- 2 cups black beans, uncooked
- 1 small red onion, peeled and diced
- 1 medium red bell pepper, diced
- ½ bunch of cilantros, chopped
- 1 lime, juiced and zested

Method:

1. Switch on the instant pot, add onion and 1 ½ teaspoon minced garlic in the inner pot along with chopped cilantro stems, sprinkle with 2 tablespoons water, press the sauté/simmer button, then adjust cooking time to 5 minutes and let cook or until vegetables are tender.
2. Add red bell pepper, season with 1 teaspoon salt, 1 tablespoon cumin, ½ teaspoon cayenne pepper, 2 tablespoon red chili powder and continue cooking for 2 minutes.
3. Add beans, pour in 3 cups vegetable broth, stir well and add water until it is 1-inch above the beans.
4. Press the cancel button, secure instant pot with its lid in the sealed position, then press the manual button, adjust cooking time to 30 minutes, select high-pressure cooking and let cook until instant pot buzz.
5. Instant pot will take 10 minutes or more to build pressure, and when it buzzes, press the cancel button and do natural pressure release for 10 minutes or more until pressure knob drops down.
6. Then carefully open the instant pot, puree the soup using an immersion blender until smooth and ladle into bowls.
7. Serve straight away.

Nutrition Value:

- Calories: 116 Cal
- Carbs: 20 g
- Fat: 1.5 g
- Protein: 5.6 g
- Fiber: 4.4 g

Millet and Bean Chili

Preparation time: 5 minutes
Cooking time: 45 minutes
Servings: 6

Ingredients:

- 2 cups pinto beans, soaked for 3 hours
- 1 cup millet, uncooked
- 1 cup fresh mixed greens
- 2 cups diced tomatoes, fire-roasted
- 1 medium red bell pepper, chopped

Method:

1. Switch on the instant pot, grease the inner pot with 1 tablespoon olive oil, press the sauté/simmer button, then adjust cooking time to 5 minutes and let preheat.
2. Add red bell pepper and 1 teaspoon minced garlic, cook for 5 minutes, then season with 1 ½ teaspoon sea salt, 2 tablespoons red chili powder, 1 teaspoon paprika and 1/2 teaspoon red chili flakes, stir until mixed and cook for 1 minute.
3. Pour in 6 cups vegetable stock, stir until mixed and press the cancel button.
4. Secure instant pot with its lid in the sealed position, then press the manual button, adjust cooking time to 33 minutes, select high-pressure cooking and let cook until instant pot buzz.
5. Instant pot will take 10 minutes or more to build pressure, and when it buzzes, press the cancel button and do quick pressure release until pressure knob drops down.
6. Then carefully open the instant pot, season with sugar, add greens and vinegar and stir until combined.
7. Serve straight away.

Nutrition Value:

- Calories: 237.4 Cal
- Carbs: 45.4 g
- Fat: 2.5 g
- Protein: 11.1 g
- Fiber: 10.3 g

Vegetable Barley Soup

Preparation time: 5 minutes
Cooking time: 30 minutes
Servings: 4

Ingredients:

- ½ cup pearled barley, uncooked
- 1 cup sliced leeks
- 1 ½ cups sliced carrots
- 2 cups sliced celery
- 3 cups mushrooms, sliced

Method:

1. Switch on the instant pot, place all the ingredients in the inner pot, season with 1 teaspoon salt, 1 tablespoon Italian seasoning and ¼ teaspoon black pepper, pour in 5 cups vegetable stock and stir until mixed.
2. Secure instant pot with its lid in the sealed position, then press the soup button, adjust cooking time to 30 minutes, select high-pressure cooking and let cook until instant pot buzz.
3. Instant pot will take 10 minutes or more to build pressure, and when it buzzes, press the cancel button and do natural pressure release for 10 minutes or more until pressure knob drops down.
4. Then carefully open the instant pot, stir the soup and ladle into bowls.
5. Serve straight away.

Nutrition Value:

- Calories: 52 Cal
- Carbs: 11 g
- Fat: 0 g
- Protein: 2 g
- Fiber: 2 g

Potato Corn Chowder

Preparation time: 10 minutes
Cooking time: 15 minutes
Servings: 6

Ingredients:

- 1 cup diced white onion
- 1 cup diced carrots
- 1 cup diced celery
- 6 cups diced potatoes
- 1/2 cup cashew cream

Method:

1. Switch on the instant pot, grease the inner pot with 1 tablespoon olive oil, press the sauté/simmer button, then adjust cooking time to 5 minutes and let preheat.
2. Add onion, cook for 3 minutes, then add 1 teaspoon minced garlic and cook for 1 minute or until fragrant.
3. Add carrot and celery, cook for 3 minutes or until vegetable begin to soften, then season with 1 teaspoon salt and ½ teaspoon black pepper, pour in 4 cups vegetable broth and stir until mixed.
4. Press the cancel button, secure instant pot with its lid in the sealed position, then press the manual button, adjust cooking time to 4 minutes, select high-pressure cooking and let cook until instant pot buzz.
5. Instant pot will take 10 minutes or more to build pressure, and when it buzzes, press the cancel button and do quick pressure release until pressure knob drops down.
6. Then carefully open the instant pot, stir in cashew cream and serve straight away.

Nutrition Value:

- Calories: 243 Cal
- Carbs: 44 g
- Fat: 5 g
- Protein: 8 g
- Fiber: 7 g

Chickpea Potato Soup

Preparation time: 10 minutes
Cooking time: 15 minutes
Servings: 2

Ingredients:

- 1 large potato, peeled and cubed
- 1 ¼ cups cooked chickpeas
- 2 cups baby spinach leaves
- 3/4 cup diced carrots
- 1/2 of white onion, peeled and chopped

Method:

1. Switch on the instant pot, pour the 1/4 cup vegetable broth in the inner pot, press the sauté/simmer button, then adjust cooking time to 5 minutes and let preheat.
2. Add onion and 1 ½ teaspoon garlic, cook for 3 minutes or until golden, then season with 3/4 teaspoon salt, 1/2 teaspoon dried oregano, 1/2 teaspoon dried thyme, and 1/4 teaspoon cinnamon and stir well.
3. Add remaining ingredients except for spinach and stir well.
4. Pour in 1 cup water, 1/2 cup coconut milk
5. Press the cancel button, secure instant pot with its lid in the sealed position, then press the manual button, adjust cooking time to 5 minutes, select high-pressure cooking and let cook until instant pot buzz.
6. Instant pot will take 10 minutes or more to build pressure, and when it buzzes, press the cancel button and do natural pressure release for 10 minutes or more until pressure knob drops down.
7. Then carefully open the instant pot, fold in spinach, press the sauté/simmer button and cook for 1 minute.
8. Add cashew cream if needed, stir well until combined and drizzle with lemon juice.
9. Serve straight away.

Nutrition Value:

- Calories: 157 Cal
- Carbs: 27 g
- Fat: 2 g
- Protein: 7 g
- Fiber: 7 g

Lentil Chili

Preparation time: 10 minutes
Cooking time: 25 minutes
Servings: 4

Ingredients:

- 2 cups green lentils
- 2 medium carrots, chopped
- 15-ounce crushed tomatoes
- 28-ounce diced tomatoes, fire-roasted
- 1 medium white onion, peeled and chopped

Method:

1. Switch on the instant pot, grease the inner pot with 1 tablespoon olive oil, press the sauté/simmer button, then adjust cooking time to 5 minutes and let preheat.
2. Add onion and 2 teaspoons minced garlic along with carrots and cook for 5 minutes or until soft.
3. Season with 3/4 teaspoon salt, 1 1/2 tablespoons red chili powder, 1 tablespoon cumin, 1/2 teaspoon ground coriander and 1 teaspoon dried oregano, pour in 4 cups vegetable broth and stir until mixed.
4. Press the cancel button, secure instant pot with its lid in the sealed position, then press the manual button, adjust cooking time to 15 minutes, select high-pressure cooking and let cook until instant pot buzz.
5. Instant pot will take 10 minutes or more to build pressure, and when it buzzes, press the cancel button and do quick pressure release until pressure knob drops down.
6. Then carefully open the instant pot, stir the chili, garnish with cilantro and drizzle with lime juice.
7. Serve straight away.

Nutrition Value:

- Calories: 342 Cal
- Carbs: 62.6 g
- Fat: 4 g
- Protein: 19 g
- Fiber: 11.6 g

Chapter 7: Beans and Grains

Millet Pilaf

Preparation time: 10 minutes
Cooking time: 10 minutes
Servings: 4

Ingredients:

- 1 cup millet, uncooked
- 8 dried apricots, chopped
- 1/4 cup shelled pistachios, chopped
- 1 1/2 tablespoons olive oil
- 1 lemon, juiced and zested

Method:

1. Switch on the instant pot, place millet and 1 ¾ cup water in the inner pot and stir until mixed.
2. Secure instant pot with its lid in the sealed position, then press the manual button, adjust cooking time to 10 minutes, select high-pressure cooking and let cook until instant pot buzz.
3. Instant pot will take 10 minutes or more to build pressure, and when it buzzes, press the cancel button and do natural pressure release for 10 minutes or more until pressure knob drops down.
4. Then carefully open the instant pot, add remaining ingredients, season with ¾ teaspoon salt and ½ teaspoon ground black pepper, and stir until mixed.
5. Garnish with parsley and serve straight away.

Nutrition Value:

- Calories: 308 Cal
- Carbs: 46 g
- Fat: 11 g
- Protein: 7 g
- Fiber: 6 g

Spiced Quinoa and Cauliflower Rice Bowls

Preparation time: 15 minutes
Cooking time: 15 minutes
Servings: 8

Ingredients:

- 12-ounces tofu, extra-firm, drained and ½ inch cubes
- 1 cup quinoa, uncooked
- 2 medium red bell peppers, chopped
- 1 large white onion, peeled and chopped
- 4 cups cauliflower rice

Method:

1. Switch on the instant pot, grease the inner pot with 1 tablespoon olive oil, press the sauté/simmer button, then adjust cooking time to 5 minutes and let preheat.
2. Add onion, cook for 3 minutes, then add 1 teaspoon minced garlic, and quinoa and cook for 2 minutes or until lightly toasted.
3. Then season quinoa with 1 teaspoon salt, ½ teaspoon ground black pepper, 1 teaspoon ground turmeric, 1 teaspoon ground cumin, and 1 teaspoon ground coriander, stir until mixed and cook for 1 minute or until fragrant.
4. Stir in 2 tablespoons vegetable broth, add tofu and red bell pepper, pour in 2 cups vegetable broth and stir until just mixed.
5. Press the cancel button, secure instant pot with its lid in the sealed position, then press the manual button, adjust cooking time to 1 minute, select high-pressure cooking and let cook until instant pot buzz.
6. Instant pot will take 10 minutes or more to build pressure, and when it buzzes, press the cancel button, do natural pressure release for 5 minutes and then do quick pressure release until pressure knob drops down.
7. Then carefully open the instant pot, add cauliflower rice along with remaining ingredients, reserving lemon juice, cilantro, and almonds, and stir until mixed.
8. Shut instant pot with the lid and let the mixture sit for 5 minutes or until cauliflower rice is tender-crisp.
9. Garnish with cilantro and almonds, drizzle with lemon juice and serve.

Nutrition Value:

- Calories: 211 Cal
- Carbs: 21.3 g
- Fat: 8.2 g

- Protein: 11.2 g
- Fiber: 10 g

Black Beans and Rice

Preparation time: 10 minutes
Cooking time: 40 minutes
Servings: 8

Ingredients:

- 1 ½ cup brown rice
- 1 ½ cup dried black beans
- ½ medium white onion, peeled and chopped
- 2 tablespoons minced garlic

Method:

1. Switch on the instant pot, grease the inner pot with 2 teaspoons olive oil, press the sauté/simmer button, then adjust cooking time to 5 minutes and let preheat.
2. Add onion, cook for 3 minutes, then add garlic, season with 1 ¾ teaspoon salt, 2 teaspoon red chili powder, 1 ½ teaspoon paprika, 2 teaspoon ground cumin, and 1 ½ teaspoon dried oregano and cook for 1 minute or until fragrant.
3. Add beans and rice, pour in 3 cups water and 3 cups vegetable broth and stir until mixed.
4. Press the cancel button, secure instant pot with its lid in the sealed position, then press the manual button, adjust cooking time to 30 minutes, select high-pressure cooking and let cook until instant pot buzz.
5. Instant pot will take 10 minutes or more to build pressure, and when it buzzes, press the cancel button and do natural pressure release for 10 minutes or more until pressure knob drops down.
6. Then carefully open the instant pot, fluff the rice with a fork, drizzle with lime juice, and serve with salsa.

Nutrition Value:

- Calories: 268 Cal
- Carbs: 39.3 g
- Fat: 9 g
- Protein: 10.3 g
- Fiber: 10.6 g

Chickpea Curry

Preparation time: 10 minutes
Cooking time: 17 minutes
Servings: 6

Ingredients:

- 30-ounce cooked chickpeas
- 1 cup corn, frozen
- 14.5-ounce diced tomatoes
- 1 medium white onion, peeled and diced
- 1 cup kale leaves

Method:

1. Switch on the instant pot, grease the inner pot with 2 tablespoons olive oil, press the saute/simmer button, then adjust cooking time to 5 minutes and let preheat.
2. Add onion, cook for 4 minutes or until softened, then add bell pepper and 1 tablespoon minced garlic and cook for 2 minutes.
3. Season with 1 tablespoon curry powder, 1 teaspoon sea salt and 1/4 teaspoon ground black pepper, continue cooking for 30 seconds, then add remaining ingredients, pour in ½ cup tomato juice and 1 cup vegetable broth and stir until mixed.
4. Press the cancel button, secure instant pot with its lid in the sealed position, then press the manual button, adjust cooking time to 5 minutes, select high-pressure cooking and let cook until instant pot buzz.
5. Instant pot will take 10 minutes or more to build pressure, and when it buzzes, press the cancel button and do natural pressure release for 10 minutes or more until pressure knob drops down.
6. Then carefully open the instant pot, stir the curry, then drizzle with lime juice and top with cilantro.
7. Serve straight away.

Nutrition Value:

- Calories: 119 Cal
- Carbs: 18 g
- Fat: 5 g
- Protein: 2 g
- Fiber: 2 g

Split Pea Soup

Preparation time: 10 minutes
Cooking time: 20 minutes
Servings: 4

Ingredients:

- 2 cups yellow split peas, uncooked
- 1 medium white onion, peeled and diced
- 2 stalks celery, sliced
- 3 medium carrots, sliced
- 1 ½ teaspoon minced garlic

Method:

1. Switch on the instant pot, grease the inner pot with 1 tablespoon olive oil, press the sauté/simmer button, then adjust cooking time to 5 minutes and let preheat.
2. Add onion, cook for 1 minute, then add carrot, garlic, and celery and cook for 2 minutes or until sauté.
3. Season vegetables with 1 teaspoon salt, 1 teaspoon ground cumin, 1/2 teaspoon ground coriander, and 2 teaspoons curry powder, stir until mixed and pour in 2 cups water and 4 cups vegetable broth.
4. Press the cancel button, secure instant pot with its lid in the sealed position, then press the manual button, adjust cooking time to 10 minutes, select high-pressure cooking and let cook until instant pot buzz.
5. Instant pot will take 10 minutes or more to build pressure, and when it buzzes, press the cancel button and do natural pressure release for 10 minutes or more until pressure knob drops down.
6. Then carefully open the instant pot, stir the soup, garnish with parsley and serve.

Nutrition Value:

- Calories: 158 Cal
- Carbs: 26 g
- Fat: 2.8 g
- Protein: 8.3 g
- Fiber: 5 g

Spanish Rice

Preparation time: 10 minutes
Cooking time: 20 minutes
Servings: 6

Ingredients:

- 1½ cups white rice, rinsed
- 1 small onion, peeled and chopped
- 1 ½ cups mixed bell pepper, diced
- 1 medium tomato, seeded and diced
- 6-ounce tomato paste

Method:

1. Switch on the instant pot, grease the inner pot with 1 tablespoon olive oil, press the sauté/simmer button, then adjust cooking time to 5 minutes and let preheat.
2. Add onion, 1 teaspoon minced garlic and all the pepper, cook for 3 minutes, then season with ¾ teaspoon salt, ½ teaspoon red chili powder and ¼ teaspoon ground cumin, pour in 2 cups vegetable broth and stir until mixed.
3. Press the cancel button, secure instant pot with its lid in the sealed position, then press the manual button, adjust cooking time to 10 minutes, select high-pressure cooking and let cook until instant pot buzz.
4. Instant pot will take 10 minutes or more to build pressure, and when it buzzes, press the cancel button and do natural pressure release for 10 minutes or more until pressure knob drops down.
5. Then carefully open the instant pot, fluff the rice with a fork, sprinkle with parsley and serve.

Nutrition Value:

- Calories: 211 Cal
- Carbs: 41 g
- Fat: 3.6 g
- Protein: 4.6 g
- Fiber: 2.7 g

Spiced Brown Rice

Preparation time: 10 minutes
Cooking time: 22 minutes
Servings: 3

Ingredients:

- 1 1/2 cups brown rice
- 1/2 cup chopped apricots, dried
- 1/2 cup cashews, roasted
- 1/2 cup raisins

Method:

1. Switch on the instant pot, place all the ingredients in the inner pot, sprinkle with 2 teaspoons grated ginger, 1/2 teaspoon cinnamon and 1/8 teaspoon ground cloves, pour in 3 cups water and stir until mixed.
2. Secure instant pot with its lid in the sealed position, then press the manual button, adjust cooking time to 22 minutes, select high-pressure cooking and let cook until instant pot buzz.
3. Instant pot will take 10 minutes or more to build pressure, and when it buzzes, press the cancel button and do natural pressure release for 10 minutes or more until pressure knob drops down.
4. Then carefully open the instant pot, fluff the rice with a fork and garnish with cashews.
5. Serve straight away.

Nutrition Value:

- Calories: 216 Cal
- Carbs: 45 g
- Fat: 2 g
- Protein: 5 g
- Fiber: 3.5 g

Salsa Brown Rice and Kidney Beans

Preparation time: 10 minutes
Cooking time: 25 minutes
Servings: 4

Ingredients:

- 1 1/2 cup brown rice, uncooked
- 1 1/4 cup red kidney beans, uncooked
- ½ bunch of cilantros, chopped
- 1 cup tomato salsa

Method:

1. Switch on the instant pot, add brown rice and beans in the inner pot, pour in 2 cups water and 3 cups vegetable stock, then add salsa and chopped cilantro stems, don't stir.
2. Secure instant pot with its lid in the sealed position, then press the manual button, adjust cooking time to 25 minutes, select high-pressure cooking and let cook until instant pot buzz.
3. Instant pot will take 10 minutes or more to build pressure, and when it buzzes, press the cancel button and do natural pressure release for 10 minutes or more until pressure knob drops down.
4. Then carefully open the instant pot, stir the beans-rice mixture, garnish with cilantro and serve.

Nutrition Value:

- Calories: 218.2 Cal
- Carbs: 37 g
- Fat: 4.3 g
- Protein: 10.4 g
- Fiber: 9.3 g

Walnut Lentil Tacos

Preparation time: 10 minutes
Cooking time: 25 minutes
Servings: 12

Ingredients:

- 1 cup brown lentils, uncooked
- 1 medium white onion, peeled and diced
- 15-ounce diced tomatoes, fire-roasted
- 3/4 cup chopped walnuts

Method:

1. Switch on the instant pot, grease the inner pot with 1 tablespoon olive oil, press the sauté/simmer button, then adjust cooking time to 5 minutes and let preheat.
2. Add onion and ½ teaspoon minced garlic, cook for 4 minutes, then season with 1/2 teaspoon salt, 1/4 teaspoon ground black pepper, 1/4 teaspoon oregano, 1 tablespoon red chili powder, 1/2 teaspoon paprika, 1/4 teaspoon red pepper flakes, 1 1/2 teaspoon ground cumin and stir until mixed.
3. Pour in 2 ¼ cups vegetable broth, press the cancel button, secure instant pot with its lid in the sealed position, then press the manual button, adjust cooking time to 15 minutes, select high-pressure cooking and let cook until instant pot buzz.
4. Instant pot will take 10 minutes or more to build pressure, and when it buzzes, press the cancel button, do natural pressure release for 5 minutes and then do quick pressure release until pressure knob drops down.
5. Then carefully open the instant pot, stir the lentils, then spoon in the tortillas, top with lettuce and jalapeno and serve.

Nutrition Value:

- Calories: 157.5 Cal
- Carbs: 25 g
- Fat: 4 g
- Protein: 6.5 g
- Fiber: 8.1 g

Citrusy Black Beans

Preparation time: 10 minutes
Cooking time: 15 minutes
Servings: 4

Ingredients:

- 2½ cups black beans, uncooked
- 1 medium white onion, peeled and chopped
- 2 teaspoons minced garlic
- 1 lime, juiced

Method:

1. Switch on the instant pot, add all the ingredients in the inner pot, season with 1 teaspoon salt, 1 teaspoon red chili flakes, 1 teaspoon dried mint, 1 teaspoon ground cumin and coriander, pour in 3 cups vegetable stock and stir until mixed.
2. Secure instant pot with its lid in the sealed position, then press the manual button, adjust cooking time to 25 minutes, select high-pressure cooking and let cook until instant pot buzz.
3. Instant pot will take 10 minutes or more to build pressure, and when it buzzes, press the cancel button and do natural pressure release for 10 minutes or more until pressure knob drops down.
4. Then carefully open the instant pot, stir the beans, drizzle with lime juice, and serve.

Nutrition Value:

- Calories: 227 Cal
- Carbs: 41 g
- Fat: 1 g
- Protein: 15 g
- Fiber: 15 g

Chapter 8: Vegetable Mains

Tofu Curry

Preparation time: 5 minutes
Cooking time: 10 minutes
Servings: 4

Ingredients:

- 14-ounce extra-firm and drained tofu, cut into cubes
- 3 tablespoons green curry paste
- 1 medium green bell pepper, cored and 1-inch cubed
- 1 cup broccoli florets
- 1 medium carrot, peeled and sliced

Method:

1. Switch on the instant pot, grease the inner pot with 2tablespoons olive oil, press the sauté/simmer button, then adjust cooking time to 5 minutes and let preheat.
2. Add green curry paste, cook for 30 seconds or until fragrant, then pour in 2 cups coconut milk and stir until mixed.
3. Add remaining ingredients, stir until mixed and press the cancel button.
4. Secure instant pot with its lid in the sealed position, then press the manual button, adjust cooking time to 2 minutes, select low-pressure cooking and let cook until instant pot buzz.
5. Instant pot will take 10 minutes or more to build pressure, and when it buzzes, press the cancel button and do quick pressure release until pressure knob drops down.
6. Then carefully open the instant pot, stir the curry, then drizzle with lemon juice and garnish with basil leaves.
7. Serve straight away.

Nutrition Value:

- Calories: 418 Cal
- Carbs: 17.8 g
- Fat: 36.8 g
- Protein: 11 g
- Fiber: 5 g

Pumpkin Walnut Chili

Preparation time: 10 minutes
Cooking time: 30 minutes
Servings: 4

Ingredients:

- 2 cups red lentils, uncooked
- 28-ounce cooked black beans
- 28-ounce fire-roasted tomatoes
- 1 ½ teaspoon minced garlic
- 2 cups walnuts, chopped

Method:

1. Switch on the instant pot, grease the inner pot, add all the ingredients, then add 3 chopped chipotle pepper, 2 chopped poblano pepper, 1 ½ teaspoon minced garlic, season with 1 tablespoon salt, 2 tablespoons red chili powder, 1 tablespoon smoke paprika and stir until mixed.
2. Pour in 6 cups water, except for pumpkin puree and beans and stir until mixed.
3. Secure instant pot with its lid in the sealed position, then press the soup button, adjust cooking time to 30 minutes, select high-pressure cooking and let cook until instant pot buzz.
4. Instant pot will take 10 minutes or more to build pressure, and when it buzzes, press the cancel button and do natural pressure release for 10 minutes or more until pressure knob drops down.
5. Then carefully open the instant pot, stir the chili, then add beans and 1 ½ cup pumpkin puree and stir until well mixed.
6. Serve straight away.

Nutrition Value:

- Calories: 333 Cal
- Carbs: 42.5 g
- Fat: 14 g
- Protein: 13.5 g
- Fiber: 12.7 g

Lentil Curry

Preparation time: 10 minutes
Cooking time: 23 minutes
Servings: 5

Ingredients:

- 1 1/2 cups green lentils, uncooked
- ginger
- 1 small shallot, peeled and chopped
- 14-ounce coconut milk
- 1 cup and 1 tablespoon water, divided

Method:

1. Switch on the instant pot, grease the inner pot with 1/2 tablespoon coconut oil, press the sauté/simmer button, then adjust cooking time to 5 minutes and let preheat.
2. Add shallots, 3 tablespoons grated ginger, 2 tablespoons minced garlic, and 1 tablespoon oil, cook for 2 minutes, then season with 1 teaspoon salt, 1/4 teaspoon cayenne pepper, 1/2 tablespoon coconut sugar, 3/4 teaspoon ground turmeric, 1 tablespoon and 1 teaspoon curry powder and stir until well combined.
3. Cook for 1 minute, then add lentils, pour in the milk and water and stir well.
4. Press the cancel button, secure instant pot with its lid in the sealed position, then press the manual button, adjust cooking time to 15 minutes, select high-pressure cooking and let cook until instant pot buzz.
5. Instant pot will take 10 minutes or more to build pressure, and when it buzzes, press the cancel button and do natural pressure release for 10 minutes or more until pressure knob drops down.
6. Then carefully open the instant pot, stir in lemon juice and sprinkle with cilantro.
7. Serve curry with brown rice.

Nutrition Value:

- Calories: 315 Cal
- Carbs: 59 g
- Fat: 12 g
- Protein: 7 g
- Fiber: 6 g

Pasta Puttanesca

Preparation time: 10 minutes
Cooking time: 11 minutes
Servings: 4

Ingredients:

- 4 cups penne pasta, whole-grain
- 1/2 cup Kalamata olives, sliced
- 1 tablespoon capers
- 4 cups pasta sauce
- 3 cups water

Method:

1. Switch on the instant pot, grease the inner pot, press the sauté/simmer button, then adjust cooking time to 5 minutes and let preheat.
2. Add 1 ½ teaspoon minced garlic, cook for 1 minute or until fragrant, then season with 1 ½ teaspoon salt, 1/4 teaspoon red pepper flakes and 1 teaspoon ground black pepper, add remaining ingredients and stir until mixed.
3. Press the cancel button, secure instant pot with its lid in the sealed position, then press the manual button, adjust cooking time to 5 minutes, select high-pressure cooking and let cook until instant pot buzz.
4. Instant pot will take 10 minutes or more to build pressure, and when it buzzes, press the cancel button and do natural pressure release for 5 minutes and then do quick pressure release until pressure knob drops down.
5. Then carefully open the instant pot, stir the pasta, and serve.

Nutrition Value:

- Calories: 504 Cal
- Carbs: 98 g
- Fat: 4 g
- Protein: 18 g
- Fiber: 7 g

BBQ Meatballs

Preparation time: 10 minutes
Cooking time: 10 minutes
Servings: 4

Ingredients:

- 2-pounds vegan meatballs, frozen
- 1 1/2 cups barbeque sauce, unsweetened
- 14-ounce can whole berry cranberry sauce
- 1 tablespoon cornstarch
- 1/4 cup and 1 tablespoon water

Method:

1. Switch on the instant pot, pour ¼ cup water in the inner pot, then add meatballs and cover with BBQ sauce and cranberry sauce.
2. Secure instant pot with its lid in the sealed position, then press the manual button, adjust cooking time to 5 minutes, select high-pressure cooking and let cook until instant pot buzz.
3. Instant pot will take 10 minutes or more to build pressure, and when it buzzes, press the cancel button and do natural pressure release for 5 minutes, then do quick pressure release until pressure knob drops down.
4. Then carefully open the instant pot, gently stir the meatballs, whisk together cornstarch and remaining water until smooth and add into the instant pot.
5. Press the sauté/simmer button, adjust cooking time to 5 minutes and cook until sauce thickens to the desired level.
6. Serve straight away.

Nutrition Value:

- Calories: 232.7 Cal
- Carbs: 169 g
- Fat: 15.2 g
- Protein: 7.3 g
- Fiber: 2.6 g

Lentil Sloppy Joes

Preparation time: 10 minutes
Cooking time: 22 minutes
Servings: 8

Ingredients:

- 1 cup brown lentils, uncooked
- 1 small white onion, peeled and diced
- 28-ounce crushed tomatoes
- 1 1/2 cups vegetable broth
- 2 tablespoons tomato paste

Method:

1. Switch on the instant pot, grease the inner pot with 1 tablespoon olive oil, press the sauté/simmer button, then adjust cooking time to 5 minutes and let preheat.
2. Add onion, cook for 2 minutes or until sauté, then add 1 ½ teaspoon minced garlic and cook for 2 minutes.
3. Season onions with 1 teaspoon salt, 1/2 teaspoon ground black pepper, 1 tablespoon chili powder, 1 teaspoon paprika, and 2 teaspoons dried oregano, add tomatoes and tomato paste, pour in 1 ½ cup vegetable broth and stir until mixed.
4. Press the cancel button, secure instant pot with its lid in the sealed position, then press the manual button, adjust cooking time to 12 minutes, select high-pressure cooking and let cook until instant pot buzz.
5. Instant pot will take 10 minutes or more to build pressure, and when it buzzes, press the cancel button and do natural pressure release for 10 minutes or more until pressure knob drops down.
6. Then carefully open the instant pot, stir the lentils mixture, and serve with rolls.

Nutrition Value:

- Calories: 166 Cal
- Carbs: 30 g
- Fat: 1 g
- Protein: 9 g
- Fiber: 11 g

Green Coconut Curry

Preparation time: 10 minutes
Cooking time: 15 minutes
Servings: 4

Ingredients:

- 3 medium potatoes, peeled and cubed
- 2 cups cauliflower florets
- 1/2 sliced red bell pepper
- 1 cup peas, frozen

Method:

1. Switch on the instant pot, add potatoes in the inner pot along with cauliflower and broccoli florets, red pepper and pour in ½ cup vegetable stock.
2. Secure instant pot with its lid in the sealed position, then press the manual button, adjust cooking time to 3 minutes, select high-pressure cooking and let cook until instant pot buzz.
3. Instant pot will take 10 minutes or more to build pressure, and when it buzzes, press the cancel button and do natural pressure release for 10 minutes or more until pressure knob drops down.
4. Carefully open the instant pot, stir the mixture, then season the curry with 1 teaspoon salt and 2 tablespoon green curry paste, pour in 2 cups vegetable stock and 1 cup coconut milk and stir until mixed.
5. Press the soup button, adjust cooking time to 10 minutes and cook until curry is thoroughly heated.
6. Serve straight away.

Nutrition Value:

- Calories: 145.1 Cal
- Carbs: 11.1 g
- Fat: 6.5 g
- Protein: 5.6 g
- Fiber: 1.8 g

Potato Carrot Medley

Preparation time: 10 minutes
Cooking time: 15 minutes
Servings: 6

Ingredients:

- 1 medium white onion, peeled and diced
- 4 pounds potatoes, peeled and cut into bite-size pieces
- 2 pounds carrots, peeled and diced
- 1 1/2 cup vegetable broth
- 2 tablespoons chopped parsley

Method:

1. Switch on the instant pot, grease the inner pot with 2 tablespoons olive oil, press the sauté/simmer button, then adjust cooking time to 5 minutes and let preheat.
2. Add onion, cook for 5 minutes or until sauté, then add carrots and cook for another 5 minutes.
3. Add 1 ½ teaspoon minced garlic, then season with 1 teaspoon spike original seasoning and 1 teaspoon Italian seasoning, pour in 1 ½ cup vegetable broth and stir well.
4. Press the cancel button, secure instant pot with its lid in the sealed position, then press the manual button, adjust cooking time to 5 minutes, select high-pressure cooking and let cook until instant pot buzz.
5. Instant pot will take 10 minutes or more to build pressure, and when it buzzes, press the cancel button and do natural pressure release for 10 minutes or more until pressure knob drops down.
6. Then carefully open the instant pot, stir the medley and garnish with parsley.
7. Serve straight away.

Nutrition Value:

- Calories: 356 Cal
- Carbs: 70 g
- Fat: 6 g
- Protein: 9 g
- Fiber: 11 g

Jackfruit Curry

Preparation time: 10 minutes
Cooking time: 15 minutes
Servings: 2

Ingredients:

- 1 small white onion, peeled and chopped
- 20-ounce green Jackfruit, drained
- 1 ½ cups tomato puree
- 1/2 teaspoon cumin seeds
- 1/2 teaspoon mustard seeds

Method:

1. Switch on the instant pot, grease the inner pot with 1 teaspoon olive oil, press the sauté/simmer button, then adjust cooking time to 5 minutes and let preheat.
2. Add all the seeds, cook for 1 minute or until sizzles, then add 2 red chilies and cook for 30 seconds.
3. Add onion along with 2 ½ teaspoons minced garlic and 1 ½ tablespoon grated ginger, season with 3/4 teaspoon salt, 1 teaspoon coriander powder, 1/2 teaspoon turmeric and 1/4 teaspoon ground black pepper and cook for 5 minutes or until translucent.
4. Pour in 1 cup water, stir until mixed and press the cancel button.
5. Secure instant pot with its lid in the sealed position, then press the manual button, adjust cooking time to 8 minutes, select high-pressure cooking and let cook until instant pot buzz.
6. Instant pot will take 10 minutes or more to build pressure, and when it buzzes, press the cancel button and do natural pressure release for 10 minutes or more until pressure knob drops down.
7. Then carefully open the instant pot, shred jackfruits with two forks and garnish with cilantro.
8. Serve straight away.

Nutrition Value:

- Calories: 369 Cal
- Carbs: 86 g
- Fat: 3 g
- Protein: 4 g
- Fiber: 6 g

Potato Curry

Preparation time: 10 minutes
Cooking time: 36 minutes
Servings: 5

Ingredients:

- 5 cups baby potatoes, cut into large chunks
- 2 cups green beans, cut into bite sized pieces
- 1 medium white onion, peeled and chopped
- 2 cups water
- 1 2/3 cups coconut milk

Method:

1. Switch on the instant pot, grease the inner pot with 1 tablespoon olive oil, press the sauté/simmer button, then adjust cooking time to 5 minutes and let preheat.
2. Add onion, cook for 5 minutes, add garlic, cook for 1 minute, then add potatoes, 2 tablespoons minced garlic, season with 2 teaspoons salt, 1 teaspoon black pepper, 1 tablespoon sugar, 1 teaspoon red chili flakes and 2 tablespoons curry powder, pour in 2 cups water and 1 2/3 cup milk and stir well.
3. Press the cancel button, secure instant pot with its lid in the sealed position, then press the manual button, adjust cooking time to 20 minutes, select high-pressure cooking and let cook until instant pot buzz.
4. Instant pot will take 10 minutes or more to build pressure, and when it buzzes, press the cancel button and do natural pressure release for 10 minutes or more until pressure knob drops down.
5. Then carefully open the instant pot, stir the mixture, stir arrowroot powder and 4 tablespoons water until combined, add into the instant pot and stir until combined.
6. Add beans, stir well, press the sauté/simmer button, then adjust cooking time to 5 minutes and until beans are tender and gravy reaches to desired consistency.
7. Serve immediately.

Nutrition Value:

- Calories: 258 Cal
- Carbs: 49 g
- Fat: 5 g
- Protein: 7 g
- Fiber: 8 g

Vegan Butter Chicken

Preparation time: 10 minutes
Cooking time: 15 minutes
Servings: 3

Ingredients:

- 1 cup cooked chickpeas
- 1 cup soy curls, dry
- 2 cups tomato salsa
- 2 tablespoons chopped green bell pepper
- ¾ cup Cashew cream

Method:

1. Switch on the instant pot, pour tomato salsa in the inner pot, add chickpeas and soy curls, and stir until just mixed.
2. Then season with 3/4 teaspoon salt, ½ teaspoon red chili powder, ½ teaspoon paprika, and ¼ teaspoon cayenne pepper, pour in ¾ cup water and stir until mixed.
3. Secure instant pot with its lid in the sealed position, then press the manual button, adjust cooking time to 10 minutes, select high-pressure cooking and let cook until instant pot buzz.
4. Instant pot will take 10 minutes or more to build pressure, and when it buzzes, press the cancel button and do natural pressure release for 10 minutes and then do quick pressure until pressure knob drops down.
5. Then carefully open the instant pot, press the sauté/simmer button, add 1 teaspoon dried fenugreek leaves, 1 teaspoon garam masala and cashew cream and stir until mixed.
6. Bring the mixture to boil, taste to adjust seasoning and then fold in remaining ingredients until mixed.
7. Garnish with cilantro and serve.

Nutrition Value:

- Calories: 318 Cal
- Carbs: 48 g
- Fat: 6 g
- Protein: 19.2 g
- Fiber: 13 g

Ratatouille

Preparation time: 10 minutes
Cooking time: 15 minutes
Servings: 4

Ingredients:

- 2 medium zucchinis, cut into 1-inch pieces
- 1 medium eggplant, cut into 1-inch pieces
- 1 cup mixed bell peppers, diced
- 14 ounces diced tomatoes with juice
- 1 medium white onion, peeled and sliced

Method:

1. Switch on the instant pot, grease the inner pot with 1 tablespoon oil, press the sauté/simmer button, then adjust cooking time to 5 minutes and let preheat.
2. Add onion and 1 teaspoon garlic, cook for 3 minutes until softened, then add 2 tablespoons oil along with eggplant pieces and cook for 4 minutes or until sauté.
3. Add 2 tablespoons oil, then add zucchini and bell peppers and sauté for 1 minute.
4. Season with 1 ¼ teaspoon salt, ¾ teaspoon black pepper, 1 teaspoon each of dried thyme and rosemary, pour in ¼ cup vegetable broth and stir until mixed.
5. Press the cancel button, secure instant pot with its lid in the sealed position, then press the manual button, adjust cooking time to 2 minutes, select high-pressure cooking and let cook until instant pot buzz.
6. Instant pot will take 10 minutes or more to build pressure, and when it buzzes, press the cancel button and do quick pressure release until pressure knob drops down.
7. Then carefully open the instant pot, remove and discard sprigs and garnish with basil and capers.
8. Serve with cooked quinoa and bread.

Nutrition Value:

- Calories: 166 Cal
- Carbs: 19 g
- Fat: 10 g
- Protein: 4 g
- Fiber: 7 g

Chapter 9: Desserts and Beverages

Pear and Cranberry Cake

Preparation time: 10 minutes
Cooking time: 35 minutes
Servings: 6

Ingredients:

- 1 cup chopped pear
- 1/2 cup chopped cranberries, fresh
- 1 1/4 cup pastry flour, whole-wheat
- 2 tablespoons ground flax seeds
- 1/4 cup agave syrup

Method:

1. Place flour in a bowl, add 1/8 teaspoon salt, 1/2 teaspoon baking powder, 1/2 teaspoon soda, and 1/2 teaspoon cardamom and stir until mixed.
2. Pour 1/2 cup almond milk in another bowl, add agave syrup, flax seeds and 2 tablespoons oil and whisk until combined.
3. Gradually whisk in flour mixture until smooth and incorporated and then fold in pear and cranberries until mixed.
4. Take a Bundt pan, about 7-inch, grease with oil, then spoon in the prepared batter and cover the pan with a foil.
5. Switch on the instant pot, pour in 1 1/2 cups water in the inner pot, insert steamer rack and place Bundt pan on it.
6. Secure instant pot with its lid in the sealed position, then press the manual button, adjust cooking time to 35 minutes, select high-pressure cooking and let cook until instant pot buzz.
7. Instant pot will take 10 minutes or more to build pressure, and when it buzzes, press the cancel button and do natural pressure release for 10 minutes or more until pressure knob drops down.
8. Then carefully open the instant pot, take out the pan, uncover it, and slice to serve.

Nutrition Value:

- Calories: 259 Cal
- Carbs: 48 g
- Fat: 6 g

- Protein: 4 g
- Fiber: 6 g

Peach Dump Cake

Preparation time: 10 minutes
Cooking time: 15 minutes
Servings: 8

Ingredients:

- 1 cup sliced peaches, deseeded and skin on
- 21-ounce peach pie filling
- 15-ounce yellow cake mix
- ½ cup vegan butter, sliced

Method:

1. Switch on the instant pot, pour 1 cup water in the inner pot and insert trivet stand.
2. Place peach slices in a heatproof bowl that fits in the instant pot, add peach pie filling along with peaches, sprinkle with 1 tablespoon brown sugar and ½ teaspoon cinnamon and toss until well coated.
3. Top peach filling with cake mix, scatter with sliced butter, cover the bowl with aluminum foil and place on the trivet stand.
4. Secure instant pot with its lid in the sealed position, then press the manual button, adjust cooking time to 10 minutes, select high-pressure cooking and let cook until instant pot buzz.
5. Instant pot will take 10 minutes or more to build pressure, and when it buzzes, press the cancel button and do natural pressure release for 10 minutes or more until pressure knob drops down.
6. When the cake is done, carefully open the instant pot and take out the cake bowl.
7. Place the bowl under the broiler and cook for 3 to 5 minutes or until the top is nicely golden brown.
8. Serve cake with vegan ice cream.

Nutrition Value:

- Calories: 245 Cal
- Carbs: 43 g
- Fat: 7.3 g
- Protein: 2.3 g
- Fiber: 1.2 g

Apple Crisp

Preparation time: 10 minutes
Cooking time: 2 minutes
Servings: 4

Ingredients:

- 5 cups sliced apples
- 1 1/2 cups Sprouted Oat and Vanilla Chia Granola
- 2 tablespoons maple syrup
- 1/2 lemon, zested
- 1 teaspoon vanilla extract

Method:

1. Place granola in a heatproof bowl that fits into the instant pot, then add 1/4 cup coconut oil, 2 tablespoons coconut sugar, ½ teaspoon ginger, and granola mixture and stir until well combined.
2. Place apples in another bowl, add 2 tablespoons coconut sugar along with remaining ingredients, then stir until mixed and layer apples on top of granola mixture.
3. Switch on the instant pot, pour 2/3 cup water in the inner pot, insert the trivet stand and place bowl on it.
4. Secure instant pot with its lid in the sealed position, then press the manual button, adjust cooking time to 2 minutes, select high-pressure cooking and let cook until instant pot buzz.
5. Instant pot will take 10 minutes or more to build pressure, and when it buzzes, press the cancel button and do quick pressure release until pressure knob drops down.
6. Meanwhile, stir together ¾ teaspoon cinnamon and lemon zest until well mixed.
7. Then carefully open the instant pot, take out the bowl, let it sit for 5 minutes and then garnish with lemon zest-cinnamon mixture.
8. Serve immediately with coconut whipped cream.

Nutrition Value:

- Calories: 293 Cal
- Carbs: 43.1 g
- Fat: 13.3 g
- Protein: 2 g
- Fiber: 4.5 g

Carrot Cake

Preparation time: 10 minutes
Cooking time: 50 minutes
Servings: 4

Ingredients:

- 1 cup shredded carrot
- 1 cup chopped dates
- 1 1/2 cups pastry flour, whole-wheat
- 2 tablespoons ground flax seed, mixed with 1/4 cup warm water
- 1/2 teaspoon vanilla extract

Method:

1. Place flour in a bowl, add 1/4 teaspoon salt, 1/4 teaspoon ground ginger, 3/4 teaspoon baking powder, 3/4 teaspoon baking soda, 1/4 teaspoon ground allspice, 1/2 teaspoon ground cinnamon, and 1/4 teaspoon ground cardamom and stir well until mixed.
2. Pour 1/2 cup almond milk in another bowl, add flaxseed mixture along with 1/4 cup avocado and vanilla and stir well until smooth.
3. Then gradually whisk in flour mixture until smooth and incorporated batter comes together, fold in dates and carrots until mixed, then spoon the batter into a cake pan that fits into the instant pot and cover the pan with aluminum foil.
4. Switch on the instant pot, pour 1 1/2 cups water in the inner pot, insert the trivet stand and place the covered cake pan on it.
5. Secure instant pot with its lid in the sealed position, then press the manual button, adjust cooking time to 50 minutes, select high-pressure cooking and let cook until instant pot buzz.
6. Instant pot will take 10 minutes or more to build pressure, and when it buzzes, press the cancel button and do natural pressure release for 10 minutes or more until pressure knob drops down.
7. When the cake is done, carefully open the instant pot, take out the cake pan, let the cake cool for 10 minutes in the cake pan and then take it out.
8. Slice and serve.

Nutrition Value:

- Calories: 374 Cal
- Carbs: 68 g
- Fat: 9 g

- Protein: 11 g
- Fiber: 9 g

Double Chocolate Cake

Preparation time: 10 minutes
Cooking time: 1 hour and 30 minutes
Servings: 6

Ingredients:

- 1½ teaspoons ground flaxseeds, mixed with 2 teaspoons warm water
- 1 cup all-purpose flour
- ⅔ cup cocoa powder
- ½ teaspoon vanilla extract
- 1 cup almond milk, unsweetened

Method:

1. Place flour in another bowl, add cocoa powder, ½ teaspoon baking powder, ⅛ teaspoon sea salt, ¼ teaspoon baking soda, ⅔ cup coconut sugar and stir until combined.
2. Then gradually whisk this mixture into the milk and vanilla until smooth and incorporated.
3. Spoon the batter into a 6 by 3-inch springform pan and smooth the top with a spatula.
4. Switch on the instant pot, pour 1 ½ cup water in the inner pot, insert a trivet stand and place cake pan on it.
5. Secure instant pot with its lid in the sealed position, then press the manual button, adjust cooking time to 90 minutes, select high-pressure cooking and let cook until instant pot buzz.
6. Instant pot will take 10 minutes or more to build pressure, and when it buzzes, press the cancel button and do natural pressure release for 10 minutes or more until pressure knob drops down.
7. When the cake is done, carefully open the instant pot, take out the pan, and let the cake cool for 10 minutes and then chill cake in the refrigerator for 20 minutes.
8. Slice and serve.

Nutrition Value:

- Calories: 217.8Cal
- Carbs: 27.3 g
- Fat: 10.5 g
- Protein: 3.7 g

- Fiber: 2.4 g

Pumpkin Spice Cake

Preparation time: 10 minutes
Cooking time: 15 minutes
Servings: 6

Ingredients:

- 3/4 cup buckwheat flour
- ¼ teaspoon pumpkin pie spice
- 1 teaspoon apple cider vinegar
- ¼ cup pumpkin puree
- 1/3 cup almond milk, unsweetened

Method:

1. Place flour in a large bowl, add 1 teaspoon baking powder, 2 tablespoons coconut oil, ½ teaspoon vanilla extract, 1/3 cup maple syrup along with remaining ingredients and whisk until incorporated and smooth batter comes together.
2. Spoon the batter into a cake pan that fits into the instant pot and smooth the top.
3. Switch on the instant pot, pour 2 cups water in the inner pot, insert a trivet stand and place cake pan on it.
4. Secure instant pot with its lid in the sealed position, then press the manual button, adjust cooking time to 15 minutes, select high-pressure cooking and let cook until instant pot buzz.
5. Instant pot will take 10 minutes or more to build pressure, and when it buzzes, press the cancel button and do natural pressure release for 10 minutes or more until pressure knob drops down.
6. Then carefully open the instant pot, take out the pan, and let cool.
7. Slice to serve.

Nutrition Value:

- Calories: 195 Cal
- Carbs: 28.9 g
- Fat: 7.5 g
- Protein: 4.3 g
- Fiber: 5.3 g

Brown Rice Pudding

Preparation time: 10 minutes
Cooking time: 22 minutes
Servings: 6

Ingredients:

- 1 cup brown rice, rinsed
- 2 tablespoons raisins
- ¼ cup maple syrup
- ½ teaspoon vanilla extract
- 2 cups coconut milk, unsweetened

Method:

1. Switch on the instant pot, place rice in the inner pot, season with 1/8 teaspoon sea salt and ¼ teaspoon ground cinnamon, then add remaining ingredients, and stir well.
2. Secure instant pot with its lid in the sealed position, then press the manual button, adjust cooking time to 22 minutes, select high-pressure cooking and let cook until instant pot buzz.
3. Instant pot will take 10 minutes or more to build pressure, and when it buzzes, press the cancel button and do natural pressure release for 10 minutes or more until pressure knob drops down.
4. Then carefully open the instant pot, stir the pudding, and serve.

Nutrition Value:

- Calories: 170 Cal
- Carbs: 35.6 g
- Fat: 1.9 g
- Protein: 2.9 g
- Fiber: 1.3 g

Baked Apples

Preparation time: 10 minutes
Cooking time: 8 minutes
Servings: 2

Ingredients:

- 2 large red apples
- 2 teaspoons raisins
- 4 teaspoons coconut sugar
- 1 cup water

Method:

1. Wash and pat dry apples and core them with a spoon
2. Switch on the instant pot, pour water in the inner pot, insert a trivet stand, then place apples on it, sprinkle with sugar and top with raisins.
3. Secure instant pot with its lid in the sealed position, then press the manual button, adjust cooking time to 8 minutes, select high-pressure cooking and let cook until instant pot buzz.
4. Instant pot will take 10 minutes or more to build pressure, and when it buzzes, press the cancel button, do natural pressure release for 10 minutes and do quick pressure release until pressure knob drops down.
5. Then carefully open the instant pot, take out the apples, and serve.

Nutrition Value:

- Calories: 99 Cal
- Carbs: 24.3 g
- Fat: 0.2 g
- Protein: 0.4 g
- Fiber: 2.6 g

Chapter 10: Sauces

Jalapeno Hot Sauce

Preparation time: 2 minutes
Cooking time: 2 minutes
Servings: 6

Ingredients:

- 1/2-pound fresh jalapeños, destemmed and sliced
- 2 teaspoons minced garlic
- 1/4 cup agave nectar
- 1/2 cup apple cider vinegar
- 2 tablespoons lime juice

Method:

1. Switch on the instant pot, add peppers in the inner pot along with garlic, season with 2 teaspoon salt and pour in ¾ cup water.
2. Press the cancel button, secure instant pot with its lid in the sealed position, then press the manual button, adjust cooking time to 2 minutes, select high-pressure cooking and let cook until instant pot buzz.
3. Instant pot will take 10 minutes or more to build pressure, and when it buzzes, press the cancel button and do natural pressure release for 10 minutes or more until pressure knob drops down.
4. Then carefully open the instant pot, add remaining ingredients and puree using an immersion blender until smooth.
5. Serve straight away.

Nutrition Value:

- Calories: 5 Cal
- Carbs: 1 g
- Fat: 0 g
- Protein: 0 g
- Fiber: 0 g

Alfredo Sauce

Preparation time: 10 minutes
Cooking time: 10 minutes
Servings: 6

Ingredients:

- 6 cups cauliflower florets
- 3/4 cup cashews
- 4 teaspoons minced garlic
- 1 teaspoon salt
- 3 cups vegetable broth

Method:

1. Switch on the instant pot, grease the inner pot with 2 tablespoons oil, press the sauté/simmer button, then adjust cooking time to 5 minutes and let preheat.
2. Add garlic, cook for 1 minute or until fragrant, then add remaining ingredients except for salt and stir until mixed.
3. Press the cancel button, secure instant pot with its lid in the sealed position, then press the manual button, adjust cooking time to 3 minutes, select high-pressure cooking and let cook until instant pot buzz.
4. Instant pot will take 10 minutes or more to build pressure, and when it buzzes, press the cancel button and do natural pressure release for 10 minutes or more until pressure knob drops down.
5. Then carefully open the instant pot, spoon the mixture in a food processor, add salt and puree until smooth.
6. Serve sauce with cooked pasta.

Nutrition Value:

- Calories: 110 Cal
- Carbs: 10 g
- Fat: 7 g
- Protein: 5 g
- Fiber: 2 g

Buffalo Sauce

Preparation time: 5 minutes
Cooking time: 15 minutes
Servings: 10

Ingredients:

- 3 cups shredded jackfruit
- 12.3-ounce silken tofu
- ¾ cup buffalo hot sauce
- 8-ounces cream cheese, vegan
- 2 tablespoons tahini

Method:

1. Place tofu in a food processor, add remaining ingredients except for jack fruits, then add ½ teaspoon minced garlic and puree until smooth.
2. Switch on the instant pot, tip the tofu mixture in the inner pot, add jackfruit, pour in ¼ cup vegetable broth and stir well.
3. Press the sauté/simmer button, adjust cooking time to 7 minutes and bring the mixture to simmer and until thoroughly heated.
4. Transfer the mixture into a heatproof dish, then place it under the broiler and cook for 5 to 8 minutes or until done.
5. Sprinkle with dried parsley and serve straight away.

Nutrition Value:

- Calories: 153 Cal
- Carbs: 15 g
- Fat: 10 g
- Protein: 3 g
- Fiber: 1 g

Cheese Sauce

Preparation time: 5 minutes
Cooking time: 5 minutes
Servings: 8

Ingredients:

- 2 large carrots, peeled and slice in round
- 1 large potato, peeled and cubed
- 1 large sweet potato, peeled and cubed
- 1/2 cup nutritional yeast
- 1/4 cup cashews

Method:

1. Switch on the instant pot, add carrot, sweet potato and potato pieces in the inner pot and pour in 1 cup water.
2. Secure instant pot with its lid in the sealed position, then press the manual button, adjust cooking time to 5 minutes, select high-pressure cooking and let cook until instant pot buzz.
3. Instant pot will take 10 minutes or more to build pressure, and when it buzzes, press the cancel button and do quick pressure release until pressure knob drops down.
4. Then carefully open the instant pot, transfer vegetables in a food processor and puree until smooth.
5. Add 1 teaspoon garlic powder, 1 1/4 teaspoon salt, 3/4 teaspoon smoked paprika, 1/4 teaspoon turmeric powder, 1 ½ tablespoon lemon juice, 1/4 cup almond milk along with remaining ingredients and puree until creamy.
6. Serve straight away.

Nutrition Value:

- Calories: 86 Cal
- Carbs: 9 g
- Fat: 3 g
- Protein: 4 g
- Fiber: 2 g

Spaghetti Sauce

Preparation time: 10 minutes
Cooking time: 20 minutes
Servings: 12

Ingredients:

- 2 large carrots, peeled and cut into large chunks
- 2-pounds tomatoes, quartered
- 2 small white onions, peeled and quartered
- 2 cloves of garlic, peeled
- 6 ounces tomato paste

Method:

1. Switch on the instant pot, place all the ingredients in the inner pot except for tomato paste, season with 1 teaspoon sea salt, 2 teaspoons dried basil and 2 teaspoons dried oregano, and don't stir.
2. Secure instant pot with its lid in the sealed position, then press the manual button, adjust cooking time to 20 minutes, select high-pressure cooking and let cook until instant pot buzz.
3. Instant pot will take 10 minutes or more to build pressure, and when it buzzes, press the cancel button and do natural pressure release for 10 minutes or more until pressure knob drops down.
4. Then carefully open the instant pot, puree the mixture using an immersion blender until smooth.
5. Add tomato paste, stir well and serve the sauce with cooked pasta.

Nutrition Value:

- Calories: 35 Cal
- Carbs: 7 g
- Fat: 0 g
- Protein: 1 g
- Fiber: 2 g

Marinara Sauce

Preparation time: 10 minutes
Cooking time: 15 minutes
Servings: 8

Ingredients:

- 1/3 cup mushrooms
- 14-ounce diced fire-roasted tomatoes
- 1/3 cup minced red bell pepper
- 1/3 cup minced white onion
- 6-ounce tomato paste

Method:

1. Switch on the instant pot, add 2 tablespoons vegetable stock in the inner pot, press the sauté/simmer button, then add mushrooms, 1 ½ teaspoon minced garlic and tomato paste, stir well and cook for 5 minutes or until sauté and sauce begin to thick.
2. Season with 1/4 teaspoon salt, 1/4 teaspoon ground black pepper, 1 teaspoon dried basil, 1 teaspoon brown sugar, 1 teaspoon dried oregano, 1/4 cup water along with remaining ingredients and stir well until mixed.
3. Press the cancel button, secure instant pot with its lid in the sealed position, then press the manual button, adjust cooking time to 8 minutes, select high-pressure cooking and let cook until instant pot buzz.
4. Instant pot will take 10 minutes or more to build pressure, and when it buzzes, press the cancel button and do quick pressure release until pressure knob drops down.
5. Then carefully open the instant pot, puree the mixture using an immersion blender until smooth and serve the sauce with cooked pasta.

Nutrition Value:

- Calories: 68.4 Cal
- Carbs: 13.4 g
- Fat: 1.8 g
- Protein: 2.6 g
- Fiber: 3.3 g

Applesauce

Preparation time: 10 minutes
Cooking time: 5 minutes
Servings: 16

Ingredients:

- 3-pounds apples, peeled and cut into large cubes
- 3 tablespoons maple syrup
- 1 tablespoon lemon juice
- 1/4 cup water

Method:

1. Switch on the instant pot, place all the ingredients in the inner pot, season with 1/8 teaspoon salt, 1 teaspoon ground cinnamon and 1/2 teaspoon ground nutmeg and stir until mixed.
2. Secure instant pot with its lid in the sealed position, then press the manual button, adjust cooking time to 5 minutes, select high-pressure cooking and let cook until instant pot buzz.
3. Instant pot will take 10 minutes or more to build pressure, and when it buzzes, press the cancel button and do natural pressure release for 10 minutes or more until pressure knob drops down.
4. Then carefully open the instant pot, stir the sauce, let cool for 10 minutes and then puree using an immersion blender until smooth.
5. Serve straight away.

Nutrition Value:

- Calories: 51 Cal
- Carbs: 13 g
- Fat: 0 g
- Protein: 1 g
- Fiber: 2 g

Hummus

Preparation time: 10 minutes
Cooking time: 35 minutes
Servings: 12

Ingredients:

- 1-pound chickpeas, dried
- 2 cloves of garlic, peeled
- 1 large lemon juiced
- 1/4 cup olive oil
- 1/4 cup tahini

Method:

1. Switch on the instant pot, add chickpeas in the inner pot and pour in 12 cups water.
2. Secure instant pot with its lid in the sealed position, then press the manual button, adjust cooking time to 35 minutes, select high-pressure cooking and let cook until instant pot buzz.
3. Instant pot will take 10 minutes or more to build pressure, and when it buzzes, press the cancel button and do natural pressure release for 10 minutes or more until pressure knob drops down.
4. Then carefully open the instant pot, drain the beans, transfer them into a food processor and pour in 3 cups of cooking liquid from the instant pot.
5. Season with 1 teaspoon salt, 1/4 teaspoon smoked paprika and 1/2 teaspoon ground cumin and process for 1 to 2 minutes or until smooth.
6. Then slowly blend in the oil, 1 tablespoon at a time, until combined and creamy hummus comes together.
7. Tip the hummus in a bowl, sprinkle with paprika, drizzle with olive oil and serve.

Nutrition Value:

- Calories: 106 Cal
- Carbs: 6 g
- Fat: 7 g
- Protein: 2 g
- Fiber: 2 g

Conclusion

Vegan lifestyle consists of whole food and plants, and thus, it has compelling benefits like weight loss, reducing risk of heart diseases, cancer, Alzheimer's disease, and many more.

If you considering going vegan, then you are not alone. The start of a vegan diet is not easy and can be overwhelming as you won't able to devour your favorite cheese sandwich or chicken recipes. Indeed, a vegan diet is difficult for those individuals who grew up eating animal food and products regularly.

So, is it worth it? Yes, the transition to an entirely plant-based diet is so much more despite amazing health benefits. Vegans have reported their sense of taste heightened, and the nutritious vegan foods bring so much pleasure. And, just in a few weeks, vegans tend to forget animal foods and junk foods. Individuals also feel an immediate increase in their energy level when they go vegan.

Moreover, the fiber intake from the diet eliminate gas problems and improve bloating. The most significant physical change you will see along with weight loss will be your skin. Vegan diet clears the complexion, and your skin will never look better than before.

Based on all these benefits, you won't be going to go back.

Made in the USA
Coppell, TX
20 November 2019